Praise for *Christian Mystics*

"Our world is in crisis, and we need road maps that can ground us in wisdom, inspire us to action, and help us gather our talents in service of compassion and justice. This revolutionary book does just that. Matthew Fox takes some of the most profound spiritual teachings of the West and translates them into practical daily meditations. Study and practice these teachings. Take what's in this book and teach it to the youth because the new generation cannot afford to suffer the spiritual and ethical illiteracy of the past."

— ADAM BUCKO, spiritual activist and cofounder of
the Reciprocity Foundation for Homeless Youth

"Matthew Fox is a rare prophet who grasps not only religion but also science from their essential mystical side and is able to unify them movingly into an open-hearted and open-minded approach to the universe."

— NANCY ELLEN ABRAMS and JOEL R. PRIMACK,
coauthors of *The New Universe and the Human Future* and
The View from the Center of the Universe

CHRISTIAN
Mystics

OTHER TITLES BY MATTHEW FOX

CHRISTIAN
Mystics

365 Readings and Meditations

MATTHEW FOX

New World Library
Novato, California

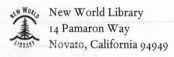

New World Library
14 Pamaron Way
Novato, California 94949

Permissions acknowledgments on page 403 are an extension of the copyright page.

Text design by Tona Pearce Myers

Library of Congress Cataloging-in-Publication Data
Fox, Matthew, date.
 Christian mystics : 365 readings and meditations / Matthew Fox.
    p.   cm.
Includes bibliographical references.
ISBN 978-1-57731-952-8 (pbk. : alk. paper)
 1. Mysticism. 2. Devotional calendars. I. Title.
BV5082.3.F69 2011
242'.2—dc22   2010049466

First printing, February 2011
ISBN 978-1-57731-952-8

Printed in Canada on 100% postconsumer-waste recycled paper

New World Library is proud to be a Gold Certified Environmentally Responsible Publisher. Publisher certification awarded by Green Press Initiative. www.greenpressinitiative.org

10 9 8 7

I dedicate this book to the young. They deserve and require a healthier version of religion, one that celebrates the depths of mysticism, love of the earth and the body, and a fierce commitment to community, compassion, celebrative rituals, and justice-making. They deserve a religion that is both simpler and more open to wisdom from all the world's spiritual traditions.

May the mystics and meditations in these pages assist us all in re-awakening the depths of our faith traditions, whatever they may be. May we travel lighter but stronger into a future worthy of our nobility as a species and worthy of the beauty of this wounded planet.

The experience of God should not be restricted
to the few or to the old.

— Thomas Aquinas

If Christianity cannot recover its mystical tradition and teach it,
it should just fold up and go out of business. It has nothing to offer.

— Father Bede Griffiths

The language of religion, by which I do not mean the stolen language
in which a male God ordains and imperial power radiates forth,
is the language of mysticism: I am completely and utterly in God,
I cannot fall out of God, I am imperishable.

— Dorothee Soelle

The number one obstacle to interfaith
is a bad relationship with one's own faith tradition.

— Dalai Lama

INTRODUCTION

Albert Einstein was asked toward the end of his life if he had any regrets. He answered: "I wish I had read more of the mystics earlier in my life." This is a significant confession, coming as it does from one of the greatest geniuses of the twentieth century, a man who moved beyond the modern science of Newton and ushered in a postmodern science and consciousness.

In the West the modern age — meaning the sixteenth to mid-twentieth century — was not only ignorant of but actually hostile to mysticism. As Theodore Roszak has put it, "The Enlightenment held mysticism up for ridicule as the worst offense against science and reason." Still today, both education and religion are often hostile to mysticism. Fundamentalism by definition is antimystical or distorts mysticism, and much of liberal theology and religion is so academic and left-brain that it numbs and ignores the right brain, which is our mystical brain. Seminaries teach few practices to access our mysticism. This is why many find religion so boring — it lacks the adventure and inner exploration that our souls yearn for. As St. John of the Cross said, "Launch out into the deep."

This launching into the depths — into the deep ocean of the unconscious and of the Great Self, which is connected to all things and to the Creator — often gets stymied by Western religious dogma, guilt trips, and institutional churchiness. The mystic gets starved. Patriarchal culture by itself is unable to tap into the deep feminine aspects of divine wisdom and Compassion and the heart. But the mystics, male and female, do not present a one-sided reality, as patriarchy does. The yin/yang, female/male dialectic is alive and well in the mystical tradition. God as Mother is honored along with God as Father. Through this, mystics seek wisdom, not mere knowledge.

The West remains so out of touch with its own mystical tradition that many Westerners seeking mysticism still feel they have to go east to find it. While this can work for many brave and generous individuals, it cannot work for the entire culture. Carl Jung warned us that "we westerners cannot be pirates thieving wisdom from foreign shores that it has taken them centuries to develop *as if our own culture was an error outlived*."

Is Western culture an "error outlived"? Or is there wisdom deep within our roots that can be accessed anew and that can give us strength and understanding at this critical time when so much is falling apart the world over? When climate change and destruction of the earth accelerate and so many species are disappearing, while our banking systems and economic belief systems, our forms of education and forms of worship, are failing?

I believe that there is great wisdom in our species and in Western spiritual traditions, but that this needs a new birth and a fresh beginning. As a Westerner I must begin where I stand within my own culture and its traditions. This is where these 365 meditations — one for each day of the year — come in. We in the West must take these insights into our hearts on a regular basis, allow them to play in the heart, and then take them into our work and citizenship and family and community. This is how all healthy and deep awakenings happen; they begin with the heart and flow out from there.

The crises we find ourselves in as a species require that as a species we shake up all our institutions — including our religious ones — and reinvent them. Change is necessary for our survival, and we often turn to the mystics at critical times like this. Jung said: "Only the mystics bring what is creative to religion itself." Jesus was a mystic shaking up his religion and the Roman Empire; Buddha was a mystic who shook up the prevailing Hinduism of his day; Gandhi was a mystic shaking up Hinduism and challenging the British Empire; and Martin Luther King Jr. shook up his tradition and America's segregationist society. The mystics walk their talk and talk (often in memorable poetic phraseology) their walk.

Deep down, each one of us is a mystic. When we tap into that energy we become alive again and we give birth. From the creativity that we release is born the prophetic vision and work that we all aspire to realize as our gift to the world. We want to serve in whatever capacity we can. Getting in touch with the mystic inside is the beginning of our deep service.

Today there is a genuine effort around the world at "deep ecumenism," or "interfaith," the coming together of the spiritual wisdom traditions of the world. That is a positive development. But the Dalai Lama points out that the "number one obstacle to interfaith is a bad relationship with one's own faith tradition." It is pitiful how few Christian leaders and Christian teachers (including in seminaries) know their own mystical lineage. These days, as revelations come to light about darkness in the Catholic Church, it is all the more important to pay attention to that which is true and deep and beautiful in the work of our Christian ancestors. Through the ages even to today, Christian mystics and activists have stirred hearts and souls. It is valuable at a time of church reformation and even revolution to tap into this wellspring of truth and renewal. Reading and praying the wisdom in these passages moves me deeply to embrace my mystic/prophet ancestors. I hope it helps to awaken the same in the reader.

The teachings here are universal, as all wisdom is. When I share them with my Buddhist and Jewish friends, for example, they spark profound "aha!" moments. Those who have traveled deep into their own well, into the living waters of wisdom, will find in the sources I present a common language and a common experience, and that is as it should be. Divinity is one "underground river," as Meister Eckhart teaches, and while we access different wells or traditions, still we come to common waters.

Those who have been touched by Christianity may well find here a Christianity they yearned to know but never heard of. Mystical Christianity is a very well-kept secret. It does not serve the interests of empire or patriarchy or churchness. But it is coming alive again. A very respected contemporary biblical scholar, John Dominic Crossan, points out that for Paul (the first Christian theologian and the first writer in the New Testament), "you cannot be a Christian without being a mystic." A new age is dawning, if that is the case, and none too soon. Our ancestors were mystics. We can be also.

You will meet some wonderful men and women in these pages. All are mystic/prophets who speak deeply to us today. In addition to Jesus and Paul, I have chosen to cite over two dozen other mystic/prophets. At the end of the book, I offer a brief description of each person (arranged alphabetically). Of course, there are lots more than thirty-two mystics in the history of Christianity, including Ralph Waldo Emerson, George Fox, George Herbert, and more. This is but a beginning. Along with the quotations, I have provided commentaries of my own, to help show how these mystics shed light on the significant issues in our time, and I invite the reader to respond by writing his or her commentaries as well.

Our very survival as a species today requires a deepened awareness and ongoing practice of many of the themes that occur and recur in these pages. Some of the common themes that emerge from the mystic activists I cite include the marriage of spirit and matter, the sacredness of the earth, deep ecumenism, the omnipresence of Divinity, darkness and shadow, beauty and joy, compassion and social and ecological justice, creativity, meditation, returning to the source, stillness, contemplation or calming the reptilian brain, loss and the dark night of the soul, sacred sexuality, and more.

Enjoy! Go deep. Let the wisdom here marry the wisdom in you and behold what you will give birth to! As with Mary, it may be another Christ. It may be a new expression of the Buddha nature.

Hopefully, our generation will not suffer the mystical illiteracy of the past few centuries that Albert Einstein lamented. We cannot afford to. To survive, our species must draw on the deepest gifts we possess. Mysticism is among the finest of these gifts, for mysticism is about the awe and the gratitude, the letting go and the letting be, the birthing and the creativity, and the compassion — including healing and celebration and justice making — that our world so sorely needs. The prophet or spiritual warrior is "the mystic in action," as American philosopher William Hocking observed. Every mystic is a healer. We are healers all.

CHRISTIAN
Mystics

The Kingdom of God is within you.

— Historical Jesus

THIS TEACHING REACHES deep into our own psyche and also into politics. Regarding ourselves, it raises the question: How big am I? How much of the divine life and spirit do I allow to flow in and through me, do I experience in me? How do I slow down and be still so I can feel that Spirit? The Spirit is as near as breathing in and breathing out.

Politically, Jesus is taking on all empires and all kingdoms and saying they can be idols. Those who hold keys to kingdoms and empires are not necessarily those who hold keys to what is really important. What is going on deep within is what is really going on. Do you agree? Do kingdoms and empires have a "within"? Or do living beings alone have a within?

2.

The Queendom of God is among you.

— Historical Jesus

"DO NOT LOOK HERE OR THERE," says Jesus. The queendom of God is not a thing. It is not an object. It is not something that is about to happen. It has already happened; it is among us. We have to clean up our perception to see it better, to breathe its presence among us. It is a relationship, many relationships. We are challenged to think of ourselves in relationship, rather than as objects, as me and you, self and other. Develop an among-ness consciousness. That is a relation consciousness.

We retranslate this phrase from Day 1 as "queendom" to bring in the feminine dimension to the "reign" of God. The Greek word used in the text can mean "among" as well as "within."

The Kingdom of God was the principal theme of Jesus' message throughout his adult life, and the pivotal hope of Galilean Judaism. Rule by a king was for Galilean Jews both the source of their oppression — under temporal emperors and kings — and their hope for the future — under God.... The world of Jesus made no distinction between politics and religion. The Romans not only obeyed the emperor, they worshipped him as God's son, Divi filius. Jews not only worshipped God, but believed that he ruled them and that one day his Kingdom would be the only power on earth and in heaven.

— Bruce Chilton

IN THESE OBSERVATIONS by biblical scholar Bruce Chilton, we are reminded of how political Jesus' language was when he invoked talk of the kingdom of God. He was taking on the kingdom of the Roman Empire; he knew it and his listeners knew it. This would lead not to an easy life but to an early death. Have we understood the price and depth of meaning behind this term "the kingdom of God" and what the implications are in our time of multinational corporate empires and other kinds of militant empires? Can we see beyond them and offer visions and practices of alternative kingdoms?

Part of the beauty of the concept of God's Kingdom was that it opened one's mind to see the divine hand in the natural world. A Galilean could stand under the stars, view the mountains, watch young animals gambol and recollect the words of a well-known psalm that all the Lord's creations give thanks to him and attest his eternal Kingdom to all people (Psalm 145:10–13). Divine power was already present in nature, yet only just dawning in human affairs. Jesus came out of the Jewish tradition of seeing God's immanence everywhere, in forces as simple and powerful as a mustard seed and yeast. Later, as a rabbi, he took the leap of seeing the divine Kingdom in how one person relates to another.

— Bruce Chilton

CHILTON REMINDS US that Jesus, being a Galilean, was close to the land and to the sky. His was a cosmic awareness and a religious consciousness that linked nature to Divinity and the kingdom of God to all of creation. He saw "God's immanence everywhere" — as did many of Jewish lineage. God is present in nature but struggles to be present among humans. God is not just a transcendent God or a distant deity but a presence within all of creation. Is that sense of "within-ness" part of your spiritual experiences as well? What flows from such a consciousness? Is this the way to recover the sense of the sacredness of the earth and to sustain the struggle for ecological justice?

Jesus came to see that all creation was infused with the pulse of God: "He looks on the earth and it trembles; he touches the mountains and they smoke" (Psalm 104:32). Creation was not only primordial; it was happening anew each day, moment by moment. When God turned his face away or withheld his Spirit, his creations were instantly snuffed out and crumbled to dust, while that same Spirit constantly renewed life (Psalm 104:29–30). God was capable at any time of destroying the world and creating new heavens and a new earth (Isaiah 65:17). Yet as Jesus himself said, all living things, the simplest birds, find their nurture in God (Matthew 6:26; Luke 12:24).

— Bruce Chilton

CHILTON TEACHES that Jesus saw creation happening anew every day, that the Spirit is continuously at work, even in the smallest instances of life and beauty on earth. From this awareness of God's spirit at work in nature, it was a simple step to be aware of God's spirit at work in history and in the community and in Jesus' own heart and mind. This is what is at the heart of the wisdom tradition from which Jesus comes. Wisdom is revealed in nature in a special way and in the creativity of humans who are employing spirit in their imaginations and works. Can you identify with Jesus' love of nature and his awareness of the revelations that nature provides and that human ingenuity and creativity provide?

6.

I am the light of the world.

— Canonical Jesus or Christ

THESE WORDS did not come from the lips of the historical Jesus. The historical Jesus did not talk this way about himself. But they are words from the early Christian community about the Christ experience they had. What does it mean to say that the Christ is the "light of the world"?

First, it means there is light in the world. That is important information — sometimes we are in a place that seems to be complete darkness, what the mystics call the "dark night of the soul." We might also call this the dark night of society or the dark night of our species. At such times it is very helpful to know that, despite appearances, the Christ — who is everywhere and in everything, just as photons or light waves are present in every atom in the universe — is present as light in the deepest, innermost center of things.

The "I am" is a name for the Divine One. This saying reminds us that the Divine One, the Divine Light, is everywhere and omnipresent. The Divine "I am" is there for the asking. We all carry it within ourselves just as we carry the Christ within ourselves. Wherever the Christ is, there is light. If we open ourselves to the depth in all things, the Light of God shines through us. "Believe in the light and you will become sons and daughters of light" (John 12:36).

Further, to affirm the light does not mean denying darkness. It is not to live a life of superficial positivism. For a shadow to exist it needs light. Light creates shadow, brings shadow out of things. Shadow and light coexist, just as nighttime follows day, in an endless cycle. We need both. Neither can be allowed to dominate.

Depression often occurs when darkness takes over and light seems banished. In these moments, we need to remember there is light in the world, a "light that darkness could not overpower" (John 1:5). We breathe this light in and out every moment of every day.

7.

God is voluptuous and delicious.

— Meister Eckhart

THIS SAYING, like many by Meister Eckhart, is quite surprising. We often forget the Maker of pleasure must know something about pleasure himself and herself. The voluptuousness of an orange, of a rose, of a beautiful piece of music, of a sunset, of a tantalizing meal, of the human body — the delicious symphony provided by our senses of taste, smell, touch, sight, and hearing — does not go unnoticed by the Creator of all voluptuousness.

Do you wish to have love?
If you wish to have love, then you must leave love.

— Mechtild of Magdeburg

LETTING GO IS A LESSON all the mystics teach us. Mechtild reminds us of a deep paradox: we sometimes must leave love to have love. We need to let go of everything eventually, at some time, and so we need to develop the art of letting go. We will even, Mechtild is saying, at times need to let go of love. Ask yourself: What are my experiences of letting go? What follows after that? Have I had to let go of love? Why? Under what circumstances? How did it change me, deepen me, transform me? To let go can be to grow.

From the very beginning, God loved us.
The Holy Trinity gave itself in the creation of all things
and made us, body and soul, in infinite love.
We were fashioned most nobly.

— Mechtild of Magdeburg

SOME RELIGIOUS LEADERS teach that at the beginning humans were ugly and evil and full of something called "original sin." Jesus does not teach that. Nor does Mechtild, who reminds us that we were "fashioned most nobly" from the get-go. We were loved from the beginning. And this nobility and lovability includes our body and soul. We were made, not in sin, but in "infinite love." That is a lot of love. Have you experienced this also? Do you agree with Mechtild?

Isness is God.

— Meister Eckhart

TO SEE THAT ISNESS IS GOD is to see the inherent sacredness of everything that exists. Everything that exists reveals to us something about God. It may be its beauty or its fierceness; its shape and order or its wildness; its simplicity or its complexity. To say that isness is God is to see God everywhere and in everything at its innermost core.

To say "Isness is God" also says something profound about our experience of time. Like Jesus saying "the queendom of God is among you" or "the kingdom of God is within you," Eckhart is insisting that the time for experiencing Divinity is now — not the past and not the future. Isness is the present.

Have you tasted how isness is God? Do you recognize the inherent reverence of every moment, of every being you encounter?

Split the wood — I am there;
lift the stone and you will find me there.

— Jesus

IN THIS TEACHING from the Gospel of Thomas, which is a very early text in Christianity, Christ is to be found everywhere, even under a stone, even in the splitting of wood. This is another teaching of the Cosmic Christ — that is, Christ as the "light present in all beings" and in all energy and activity in the universe. This speaks of an intimate presence as well as an omnipresence.

Here in Galilee, the Kingdom was revealed in the weaving and stitching, planting and reaping, grape picking and pressing that assured a full life, not merely survival. Those activities find their way into Jesus' parables as images of God's Kingdom in a way that contrasts with the far less organic imagery of the Essenes at Qumran and the Rabbis in Talmud.

Galileans were enormously proud of the fertility of their land, which exceeded that of other regions in Palestine. The immediate, physical life worked out on the land provided food and wine for them. The rich bounty of the green Galilean hills mirrored their hope for the Kingdom that God yearned to provide for his people.

— Bruce Chilton

JESUS WAS A PEASANT, he was of the land, and the land he was from, Galilee, was rich and green and fertile. Healthy food and hearty wine were part of the fruit of the harvest, and neither he nor his neighbors were afraid of the hard work it took to bring forth the bounty of the land. Have you lived on a farm or do you know others who have? Are they special for their communion with nature and their appreciation of earth's gifts? Jesus drew so many of his teachings from his experience on the land. His was not an urban perspective but a close-to-the-earth perspective. He probably had more in common with a Native American perspective than with an industrial worldview.

13.

God is love.

— John, Episle of John

IF GOD IS LOVE, then God is encountered in all that we love and cherish — from friends and lovers and children to sunsets and animals, panda bears and whales, dogs, cats, and zebras. If God is love, then the music I love, the poems I love, the sunshine I love, the winds I love, the landscapes I love are all theophanies, epiphanies of the Godhead. Do you see life that way? How can this transform your life?

To say that God is Love also rules out images of God as a great judge in the sky: a peeping tom in the bedroom, an avenger God out to destroy others, or the God of empires and the God of the powerful lording over the less powerful. These are not images of a God of love, and therefore they are not God but an idol.

This passage also rebuts homophobia, since the words are not "God is heterosexual love" but "God is love." All love is a taste of the Divine, and love comes in many flavors and styles and preferences.

Then the King will say to those on his right hand, "Come, you whom my Father has blessed, take for your heritage the kingdom prepared for you since the foundation of the world. For I was hungry and you gave me food; I was thirsty and you gave me drink; I was a stranger and you made me welcome; naked and you clothed me, sick and you visited me, in prison and you came to see me." Then the virtuous will say to him in reply, "Lord, when did we see you hungry and feed you; or thirsty and give you drink? When did we see you a stranger and make you welcome; naked and clothe you; sick or in prison and go to see you?" And the King will answer, "I tell you solemnly, in so far as you did this to one of the least of these brothers of mine, you did it to me.... I tell you solemnly, in so far as you neglect to do this to one of the least of these, you neglect to do it to me."

— Historical Jesus

THIS IS COSMIC CHRIST TALK from the mouth of the historical Jesus. It forms the bridge between Jesus and Christ, for here, Jesus is saying that people are not just who they seem to be; they are also another Jesus, another Christ. This is Christ mysticism; it is the Cosmic Christ being named.

Jesus goes further. He links this mysticism directly to action, to service. He personalizes compassion. To relieve the misery of "the least of these brothers" is to relieve the misery of Christ. To feed a hungry person is to feed him. Christ mysticism is not so much about tête-à-têtes with Christ as about service rendered to Christ through the least of these brothers. Jesus also speaks to inaction, to sins of omission.

This encompasses an entire ecological theology — since "the least" may include the animals, fish, birds, trees, soil, and air. The Cosmic Christ is in all things, so to bless all things is to bless the Christ; to harm things is to harm the Christ. One can say, to crucify the Christ.

Jesus uses these invitational and provocative forms of speech —
aphorisms and parables — to subvert conventional ways of seeing
and living, and to invite his hearers to an alternative way of life.
As a teacher of wisdom, Jesus was not primarily a teacher of infor-
mation (what to believe) or morals (how to behave), but a teacher
of a way or path of transformation. A way of transformation from
what to what? From a life in the world of conventional wisdom to a
life centered in God.... He directly attacked the central values of his
social world's conventional wisdom: family, wealth, honor, purity,
and religiosity. All were sanctified by tradition, and their importance
was part of the taken-for-granted world.... The transformation from
secondhand religion to firsthand religion, from living in accord with
what one has heard to life centered in the spirit, is central to the al-
ternative wisdom of Jesus and also to the Jewish tradition in which
he stood.

— Marcus J. Borg

WE SEE FROM MARCUS BORG'S OBSERVATIONS that Jesus was a
mystic, for a mystic is one who trusts "firsthand religion," that
is, experience. But Jesus' message of alternative wisdom is sub-
versive, according to Borg, for it challenges many stereotypes
of what we take for granted regarding family, wealth, honor,
purity, and religiosity itself. He taught transformation, personal
and social. Is that the Jesus you recognize? Is that the Jesus you
could follow and emulate?

He [Jesus] had both a religious dream and a social program, and it was that conjunction that got him killed. The Roman Empire may have regularly abused its power but it seldom wasted it. It did not crucify teachers or philosophers; it usually just exiled them permanently or cleared them out of Rome periodically. Indeed, if Jesus had been only a matter of words or ideas, the Romans would have probably ignored him, and we would probably not be talking about him today. His Kingdom movement, however, with its healings and exorcisms, was action and practice, not just thought and theory.

— John Dominic Crossan

CONTEMPORARY BIBLICAL SCHOLAR John Dominic Crossan underscores the kind of person Jesus was and the kind of work that Jesus did. He was not just a theoretician — his teaching had practical consequences not only for the lives of individuals but for the culture at large. He challenged the individual and the culture. That is why the Roman Empire killed him. They knew he was implicating their version of kingdom every time he taught about an alternative kingdom, the kingdom of God. What are the implications of Jesus' vision for today's world?

The Kingdom movement was Jesus' program of empowerment for a peasantry becoming steadily more hard-pressed through insistent taxation, attendant indebtedness, and eventual land expropriation, all within increasing commercialization in the expanding colonial economy of a Roman Empire under Augustan peace and a Lower Galilee under Herodian urbanization. Jesus lived, against the systemic injustice and structural evil of that situation, an alternative open to all who would accept it: a life of open healing and shared eating, of radical itinerancy, programmatic homelessness, and fundamental egalitarianism, of human contact without discrimination, and of divine contact without hierarchy. He also died for that alternative. That is my understanding of what Jesus' word and deeds were all about. And I emphasize that it involved not so much Jesus' personal power as communal empowerment and not so much an idea in the mind as a life in the body. But notice that reciprocity of eating and healing is at the heart of the Kingdom's program and presence.

— John Dominic Crossan

CROSSAN SPELLS OUT the full meaning of the kingdom of God as Jesus taught and lived it, and for which he paid the ultimate price. Jesus' strategy involved eating, meetings at table of the rich and the poor, the haves and have-nots, in order that healing of classes might take place. Crossan places Jesus in his historical context when he elsewhere describes Jesus as a "Mediterranean Jewish peasant speaking to other peasants in the dangerous location of an occupied country, in the volatile situation of increasing subjugation and in the explosive circumstances of an economy booming for the urban upper classes through increasing indebtedness, land expropriation, and destitution on the part of the rural lower classes." Do you see any similarities between Jesus' situation and today's culture? Between the peasant classes of Jesus' day and the "Main Street" of our day?

Took, blessed, broke, *and* gave *have profound symbolic connotations.... They indicate, first of all, a process of* equal sharing, *whereby whatever food is there is distributed alike to all. But they also indicate something even more important. The first two verbs* took *and* blessed, *and especially the second, are the actions of the master; the last two,* broke *and* gave, *and especially the second, are the actions of the servant. Jesus, as master and host, performs the role of servant, and all share the same food as equals. There is, however, one further step to be taken. Most of Jesus' first followers would have known about but seldom experienced being served at table by slaves. The male followers would think more experientially of females as preparers and servers of the family food. Jesus took on himself the role not only of servant but of female. Not only* servile *but* female hosting *is symbolized by the* juxtaposition *of those four verbs. Far from reclining and being served, Jesus himself serves, like any housewife, the same meal to all, including himself.*

— John Dominic Crossan

CROSSAN SPELLS OUT some of the revolutionary dimensions to Jesus' strategy of getting people of diverse classes and backgrounds to eat together, breaking down his ministry of meals. It involved equal sharing, being master who blesses and servant who serves, and hosting as the woman of a household would host, thus mixing male and female roles. All this was original on Jesus' part. All of it eventually got him in trouble. How much has been lost since these meals were ritualized as one "Last Supper" and then as worship or Mass? What can be salvaged? How would that come about?

We sink eternally from letting go to letting go into God.
— Meister Eckhart

ECKHART REMINDS US how radical and forever are our experiences of letting go. There is no stopping them. Life is a series of letting-go moments: from when we leave the womb — letting go of the comfort of nine months in our mother's belly — to the hour of our death and our final leave-taking. Every new beginning involves a letting go: when we go to our first day of school, when we graduate from high school, when we embark on a career or relationship, when we get married and leave single life and other romantic relationships behind, when we become parents. Since life is about letting go, it's good to develop the habit now and with a smile on our faces!

> *The earth is at the same time mother,*
> *she is mother of all that is natural, mother of all that is human.*
> *She is the mother of all, for contained in her are the seeds of all.*

— Hildegard of Bingen

PREMODERN THINKERS — native peoples around the world but also our medieval ancestors in Europe — honored the earth as Mother. This naming renders us in a familial relationship with the earth. Mother is bountiful and generous. She cares and she provides. That is the way of any mother, and it is surely the way of mother earth, who is, as Hildegard observes, "mother of all that is human." Are we treating her with the respect that the mother of all that is natural and the mother of all that is human deserves? Who would choose to abuse one's mother?

As the Creator loves his creation, so creation loves the creator.
Creation, of course, was fashioned to be adorned,
to be showered, to be gifted with the love of the creator.
The entire world has been embraced by this kiss.

— Hildegard of Bingen

HILDEGARD IS PICTURING an erotic relationship between creation and the creator, one that spreads to the "entire world" because the entire world "has been embraced by this kiss." How far this is from the Newtonian notion that God is up in the sky with an oilcan, keeping the mechanical universe running. Instead, God is involved intimately and sensually and erotically with creation, out of love for creation.

God has gifted creation with everything that is necessary....
Nothing that is necessary for life is lacking.

— Hildegard of Bingen

HILDEGARD IS TEACHING US to trust when she says that everything that is necessary is already within creation. When things look bleak for us, when bills go unpaid or a relationship sours, we can easily fall into despair and self-pity. But Hildegard urges us to look deeper inside. Life is what matters. All else is a detail. We have been given the gift of life, and within that gift is "everything that is necessary." This includes our creativity and imagination to overcome adversity, to forge new directions and relationships.

*Holy Spirit, you are the mighty way in which everything
that is in the heavens, on the earth, and under the earth,
is penetrated with connectedness, is penetrated with relatedness.*

— Hildegard of Bingen

INTERDEPENDENCE AND INTERRELATIONSHIP are deep ways of seeing the world that our premodern ancestors celebrated. The modern age thought in terms of subjects and objects. But today, and in Hildegard's day, the key to understanding self and others is connectedness. She points out how fundamental those ways are when she says things are "penetrated" with connectedness. Ask yourself: Am I attuned to my connection with everything that is in the heavens, on the earth, and under the earth? With all my relations? For Hildegard this is the Spirit's work: Holy Spirit is the "mighty way" of connectedness and relatedness.

24.

Relation is the essence of everything that exists.
— Meister Eckhart

CONTEMPORARY PHYSICS is arriving more and more at this awareness that Eckhart and other great mystics have sensed over the centuries. Things are not just things. There is no thing in and of itself, separately defined; the essence of thingness is not thingness — it is relationship. The insides of an atom, the moving parts, only function in relationship to each other. Further, galaxies and clusters of galaxies reveal the same truth: their existence depends on the relationship of their parts more than the parts themselves.

I, the fiery life of divine wisdom, I ignite the beauty of the plains,
I sparkle the waters, I burn in the sun, and the moon, and the stars.
With wisdom I order all rightly. Above all, I determine truth.

—— Hildegard of Bingen

HILDEGARD IDENTIFIES WISDOM with the "fiery life" that dwells in all things — not in a passive way, but in a luminous way that infuses everything with numinousness and beauty. Have you experienced what Hildegard names? In moments of natural beauty, do you see the fiery life of wisdom at work, ordering things rightly? How can you deepen that teaching, that all things are ignited with wisdom? Wisdom also brings order; wisdom honors the whole and not just the part.

Who is the Trinity? You are music. You are life. You are alive in everything, and yet you are unknown to us.... God says: I am the supreme fire; not deadly, but rather, enkindle every spark of life.

— Hildegard of Bingen

THE TEACHING THAT DIVINITY is the fire enkindling the spark of life in all things is common to all mystics; it's in the Jewish Kabbalah as well as the writings of Meister Eckhart. Here, Hildegard also calls God "music." She calls the God essence "life" itself that is alive in everything, and then insists that Divinity remains hidden, unknown, a mystery to us. Do you agree? Is God a song that we cannot hear? If so, how would you listen for it?

There is no creation that does not have radiance.
Be it greenness or seed, blossom or beauty.
It could not be creation without it.

— Hildegard of Bingen

THE THEOLOGICAL WORD for "radiance" is *doxa* in Greek, which means "glory." So the radiance that Hildegard refers to is more than just light. However, according to today's science, atoms — the building blocks of life — contain photons or light waves. This would seem to substantiate what Hildegard describes, that all creation is in a literal way light itself. Look around you: Do you find a radiance in everything you see? Can you look for it, find it, touch it in everything you see today?

It is no longer I who live but Christ who lives within me....
And we, with our unveiled faces reflecting like mirrors
the glory of the Lord, all grow brighter and brighter
as we are turned into the image that we reflect.

— Paul

IN SURRENDERING TO HIS EXPERIENCE of the Christ, Paul believes that Christ has taken over his person. Have you had an experience like that? Has God or Christ or the Buddha or another presence ever taken over your person so that he or she seems to be living within you?

Paul speaks of our "unveiled faces," or our true selves, reflecting the glory of God as something that evolves as we grow. We are not just born this way; we become "brighter and brighter" as we develop, mature, and grow spiritually into greater God-likeness.

"He is the invisible God's image, firstborn of all creation because within him everything was created...." In Colossians Christ is the center of the cosmos — natural, social and supernatural — that created the world and makes the world new each day.... The range of Paul's thinking was literally cosmic, and metacosmic.... No Christian thinker before or since has thought on so cosmic a scale, linking God's Spirit to humanity's and both to the transformation of the world. The picture he conveyed of what it meant for even small groups of believers to meet together involved them in a literal reshaping of the universe.

— Bruce Chilton

IT IS AMAZING TO LEARN from Chilton that Paul, the very first writer of the Christian Bible and the very first Christian theologian, thought more cosmically and metacosmically than any Christian thinker before or since. What an invitation to learn and integrate the new cosmology and to revivify the Christ message in that context. A time like ours, so gifted with a new cosmology, but so needing a global and ecological vision, requires a rethinking of everything in light of a cosmic awareness.

Meanwhile, John Dominic Crossan makes clear that there is no way to understand Paul except as a mystic: "For Paul being 'in Christ' is not just metaphorical trope, but mystical identity. It determines everything in his theology....Paul is a mystic. He thinks mystically, writes mystically, teaches mystically, and lives mystically. He also expects other Christians to do likewise."

How will Christianity renew itself if it does not renew its mystical tradition and teach mysticism?

A wheel was shown to me, wonderful to behold....Divinity is in its omniscience and omnipotence like a wheel, a circle, a whole that can neither be understood, nor divided, nor begun nor ended....God hugs you. You are encircled by the arms of the mystery of God.

— Hildegard of Bingen

THE CURVE OF THE UNIVERSE is very maternal, and the wheel of God is eternal and beyond understanding. What does it mean to be "encircled by the arms of the mystery of God"? Does it give you some peace to feel this embrace even when difficulties arise? Do you live your life as if it had a beginning and an ending, or as if it were an eternal undivided wheel? How important are curves and wheels in your view of life?

All praise be yours, my Lord, through all that you have made,
　　And first my Lord Brother Sun,
　　Who brings the day; and light you give to us through him.
How beautiful he is, how radiant in all his splendor!
　　Of you, Most High, he bears the likeness.

All praise be yours, my Lord through Sister Moon and Stars;
　　In the heavens you have made them bright
　　And precious and fair....

All praise be yours, my Lord, through Sister Earth, our mother,
　　Who feeds us in her sovereignty and produces
　　Various fruits and colored flowers and herbs....

All praise be yours, my Lord through Sister Death,
　　From whose embrace no mortal can escape.

— Francis of Assisi

IN THIS, HIS BEST-KNOWN POEM, Francis of Assisi underscores our rich relationship with the cosmos, in which Sun, Moon, Stars, Earth, and Death itself are named as kin: Brother, Mother, Sister. Like indigenous peoples everywhere, Francis reminds us of the integral relationship of the entire family of beings, and that the forces of the universe constitute all our relations. Among these relatives, "Lord Brother Sun" is first and most esteemed, for the sun brings life to the earth and its radiant light bears a special "likeness" to the Creator.

Do you share relationships with the cosmic powers as Francis does? Have you written a poem about them lately? What about "Sister Death"? Have you befriended her as part of a cosmically based spiritual awareness?

Francis of Assisi came before [Pope Innocent III] to plead: "I do not come here with a new rule; my only rule is the gospel." Thus did the gospel confirm its inalienable vitality and relevance, in galvanizing both human understanding and even ecclesiastical foundations. It is the common inspiration of all Christians of all times and all milieux, but its abrupt recrudescence periodically provokes a spiritual and institutional crisis, against which it is clearly preferable to measure the pace and standards of the life of the church.

— M. D. Chenu

MEDIEVAL HISTORIAN FATHER CHENU is talking about the revolution that Francis of Assisi began in the Christian church by attempting to return to Gospel values with his new order of Franciscan friars. Chenu points out how every renewal in church history is about returning to the original source and inspiration of the Jesus message and story and that this provokes spiritual and institutional crises. Do you sense such an awakening today, one provoking crises in ecclesial complacency? Are you part of such a movement?

Like St. Peter speaking to the community at Jerusalem (Acts 2:14–21), the elders of the apostolic movements took up the text of Joel on the day of the Lord: "I will pour out my spirit upon all of mankind, and your sons and daughters will be prophets. Your young men shall see visions, and your old men shall dream dreams." This prophetic attribution, common enough in tradition and liturgical anointing, had a special vigor for these generations.... Thus, one can define the evangelical reawakening as an active presence of the gospel, not only because men took up the text and read it directly in its literal fullness, but also because, at the same time, the word of God was announced as real and present by action of the Holy Spirit in a vibrant church and a revitalized theology.

— M. D. Chenu

WHILE CHENU IS SPEAKING of the reformation and renaissance of the radical Christian movements of the late twelfth and early thirteenth centuries, his words and those movements speak to our times as well. Today also, the Holy Spirit seeks "a vibrant church and a revitalized theology," and the energy comes from the prophetic spirit that goes back at least as far as the prophet Joel and the days of Peter and the early Christian movement. Do these promises, that the Spirit will be poured on all of humanity, especially the young, apply with a "special vigor" to our times as well? Are you feeling that Spirit and acting to make a vibrant religion and revitalized theology happen?

God is everything that is good
and the goodness that everything possesses is God.

— Julian of Norwich

MEISTER ECKHART SAYS that isness is God, but here Julian, who followed Meister Eckhart, reports that goodness is God. Every experience of goodness is an experience of God. Is that your experience also? Since the theological word for "goodness" is *blessing*, we could also say that every blessing is an experience of God. When you experience goodness in your life, to whom do you give credit?

*As the body is clothed in cloth and the muscles in the skin
and the bones in the muscles and the heart in the chest, so are we,
body and soul, clothed in the Goodness of God and enclosed.*

— Julian of Norwich

WE ARE CLOTHED AND ENCLOSED in the goodness of God. This image is a lot like Hildegard's of being "hugged and encircled by the arms" of God — also an enclosing. This is a very maternal and compassionate image of our relationship to Divinity. It also hints at the intimacy of the relationship. Can you imagine your own flesh and bones as the arms of God holding your heart and soul?

God showed me in my palm a little thing round as a ball about the size of a hazelnut. I looked at it with the eye of my understanding and asked myself: "What is this thing?" And I was answered: "It is everything that is created." I wondered how it could survive since it seemed so little it could suddenly disintegrate into nothing. The answer came: "It endures and ever will endure, because God loves it." And so everything has being because of God's love.

— Julian of Norwich

JULIAN SAW ALL OF CREATION in a tiny hazelnut — and she saw that it was fragile but that it endured because God loved it. God loves all of creation. Can you imagine all of creation as a single, loved entity in the palm of your hand? Tiny but immense? Microcosm of the vast macrocosm? All of it loved?

God is thirsty for everyone. This thirst has already drawn
the Holy to Joy and we the living are ever being drawn and drunk.
And yet God still thirsts and longs.

— Julian of Norwich

HAVE YOU HEARD or thought before about God's thirst? And how we help to quench it? Does the divine thirst draw you to joy? What experiences have you had of this thirst? She says we drink and we are "drawn," or drunk. Is that your experience also? Do you sense with Julian that God is longing? What is God longing for? What or whom are we longing for?

Some of us believe that God is All-Power and can do all, and that God is All-Wisdom and knows how to do all. But that God is All-Love and wants to love all, here we restrain ourselves. And this ignorance hinders most of God's lovers, as I see it.... God wants to be thought of as our Lover.

— Julian of Norwich

FOR JULIAN GOD IS NOT JUST LOVE but "All-Love." What are the implications of that awareness in our lives? Do you agree with Julian that we hinder ourselves by denying that God is All-Love? What can we do to lessen that obstacle in our self-understanding and God understanding? Do you agree that God wants to be considered our lover? How real is this for you?

I saw the Soul so large as if it were an endless world and a joyful kingdom. And I understood that it is a beautiful City. In the midst of that city sits our Lord Jesus, God and one of us, a beautiful person of large stature clothed as befits his role as Bishop and King. And beautifully he sits, peacefully and restfully, in the Soul, his most familiar home and endless dwelling.

— Julian of Norwich

IN THE MIDDLE AGES, "soul" and "city" were often considered one concept because each was an intersection for so many life energies. (In the East the word *chakra* also means "intersection" and has many rich applications.) Again, as with the image of the hazelnut, Julian plays with perspective to get our attention: Can you imagine your soul so large it contained a city, an "endless world"? How might it change your sense of self to imagine Jesus presiding over that city, sitting in your soul as if it were his familiar home and dwelling? How would it alter our view of cities to imagine all souls in them as part of one Soul?

Nature and Grace are in harmony with each other. For Grace is God and Nature is God. Neither Nature nor grace works without the other. They may never be separated.... That Goodness that is Nature is God. God is the Ground, the substance, the same that is Naturehood. God is the true Father and Mother of Nature.

— Julian of Norwich

THE SEPARATION OF NATURE AND GRACE often leaves us confused and fearful of life. When we can no longer feel the grace of nature we need to pause and allow grace to bless us again. Julian believes a separation of nature and grace is foolish and dangerous. Do you agree with her? What examples of nature as grace do you have in your life? Many theologians in the past (such as St. Augustine) have separated nature from grace, and in this way have created pessimism. Julian does not. The experience of the sun, of animals, of one's body, of another's body, of food — the truth of nature as grace goes on and on.

Julian often emphasized her belief that all goodness is God, and this includes the entirety of the natural world, including all living creatures, from birds to trees; nature itself, in the form of land and rivers; and also our own nature as human beings. All of it contains in its ground and substance God, who is "Father and Mother."

God says: "I am the sovereign goodness of all things.
I am what makes you love. I am what makes you long and desire.
This I am — the endless fulfilling of all desires."

— Julian of Norwich

GOD HAS MANY NAMES. Here Julian offers a few — the "sovereign goodness" found in all things; that which makes us love; that which makes us long and desire; "the endless fulfilling of all desires." Do you agree with Julian that God is the source of our desires and longing?

Just as God is truly our Father, so also is God truly our Mother....
The deep Wisdom of the Trinity is our Mother.
In her we are all enclosed.

— Julian of Norwich

SOME PAINT AN IMAGE OF GOD that is exclusively male. Obviously Julian was not such a person. Here Julian elaborates on her theme of God as Mother. True to ancient traditions both biblical and otherwise, she sees Wisdom (*Sophia* in Greek) as feminine — indeed, as Mother in whom all things are enclosed. Does it change your view of the Divine to see God as both feminine and masculine, Mother and Father? What are the implications for our daughters and granddaughters, for our sons and grandsons?

Our Sensuality is the beautiful City in which our Lord Jesus sits and in which He is enclosed....In our sensuality God is.

— Julian of Norwich

JULIAN CELEBRATES OUR SENSUALITY. She is not saying we must repress or drive away our sensuality for God to be present within us — quite the opposite. She sees our sensuality as the "beautiful City" in which Christ sits and is enclosed.

By honoring the nearness of God to our sensuality, Julian takes on all those ascetic teachers who say we have to run from our senses to experience Divinity. God is present in our sensuousness, and this characterization ends the Platonic dualisms — the body versus soul warfare — that have haunted patriarchal religion and philosophy for twenty-five hundred years.

> *God is nearer to us than our own soul and God is*
> *the means whereby our Substance and our Sensuality*
> *are kept together so as to never be apart.*

— Julian of Norwich

HOW CLOSE IS GOD TO US? Nearer than we are to ourselves, Julian is saying. But what does this mean? Julian imagines God as a kind of glue holding our substance, or our soul, together with our senses and sensuality. So pleased is God with our true nature as sensuous animals that God plays the role of intermediary between our soul and our senses.

I saw that God never began to love us....
We have always been in God's foreknowledge, known and loved
from without beginning.... We were made for love.

— Julian of Norwich

To SAY WE HAVE BEEN "loved from without beginning" is to speak of original blessing rather than original sin. Julian breaks with Augustine and others who have preached about an original sin, and she sides with all those who know we have been loved before the beginning.

Do you agree with Julian that we were made for love? How are we doing? What levels and kinds of love have you tasted? What do you still have to learn about love?

We are in God and God whom we do not see is in us.

— Julian of Norwich

JULIAN HERE CELEBRATES the reality of panentheism: God in us and us in God. But she underscores how this is not always clear, since we do not see God. Notice how different panentheism is from theism. The latter says, "We are here and God is out there someplace." Panentheism names the nearness of God, we in God and God in us, like the fish in the water and the water in the fish. That is how grace operates. Panentheism is the mystical way of understanding our relationship to Divinity.

God feels great delight to be our Father and God feels great delight to be our Mother and God feels great delight to be our true Spouse and our soul the loved Wife. Christ feels great delight that he is our Brother and Jesus feels great delight that He is our Liberator. These are five great joys that God wants us to enjoy.

— Julian of Norwich

JULIAN, LIKE ECKHART AND AQUINAS, talks about the delight of God and the joy of God and how we share in both. God takes "great delight" in being Father, Mother, Spouse, Brother, Liberator. Do we feel these five aspects of God's delight and relationship to us? Try meditating on each of these five roles of God — and remember, in Julian's words, each one is a "great joy" that God urges us to enjoy.

I saw no kind of vengeance in God.
In God are endless friendship, space, life and being....
I saw wrath and vengeance only on our part.
God forgives that in us.

— Julian of Norwich

GOD IS NOT A PUNITIVE, vengeful, or wrathful God for Julian. Instead, God contains "endless friendship, space, life and being." For Julian it is we who are wrathful and vengeful, not God. How does this alter, clean up, or detox your understanding of Divinity? What difference does that make to our reading and understanding of human history? What kind of healing medicine is contained in this understanding of God?

Our soul must perform two duties.
The one is we must reverently wonder and be surprised;
the other is we must gently let go
and let be always taking pleasure in God.

— Julian of Norwich

HERE JULIAN NAMES the via positiva and the via negativa paths of creation spirituality. The first is to wonder and be open to awe and surprise; the second is to let go and let be. These are the first steps of the spiritual path. How are we as a society doing? How are you doing?

The next two paths of the creation spirituality journey are the via creativa, or creativity, and the via transformativa, or justice and compassion. But they flow from these first two paths of praise and of the letting go, which we learn from silence and from suffering.

God is the goodness that cannot be wrathful.
Our soul is oned to God, unchangeable goodness,
and therefore between God and our soul there is neither wrath
nor forgiveness because there is no between.

— Julian of Norwich

JULIAN DECLARES that there "is no between" separating God and us. This is a profound and stark way of talking about the nondualism, the authentic communion between us and Divinity. Have you had glimpses of that union, that nondualism, that "oneing" between yourself and God?

True thanking is to enjoy God.

— Julian of Norwich

THANKING AND ENJOYMENT go together. Think of it. If you give someone a gift and they do not use it, then you will feel disappointment, despite any genuinely nice thank-you note they may write. If you give them a gift that they enjoy using, that joy is the most satisfying thank-you they could offer. Their joy makes us happy. So, too, in Julian's view, we thank God more by our enjoyment of God's gifts than through mere words. And this delights God.

*If the only prayer you say in your whole life is
"Thank You," that would suffice.*

— Meister Eckhart

MEISTER ECKHART, like Julian, believes that gratitude is at the heart of an authentic spiritual existence. In fact, prayer is for him primarily an act not of begging or beseeching or wanting or needing — but of thanking. The word *eucharist* comes from the Greek word for "to give thanks." So Christian worship is primarily a thank-you gathering. Thomas Aquinas also taught that the very essence of true religion is gratitude.

*Often our trust is not full. We are not certain that God hears
us because we consider ourselves worthless and as nothing.
This is ridiculous and the cause of our weakness.
I have felt this way myself.*

— Julian of Norwich

JULIAN ADMITS TO HER OWN FAILURES in trust and her own
self-doubts and feelings of worthlessness. Most of us have these
feelings at times. But she eschews them; she urges us to go beyond them. For Julian, trust is everything. And trust (more than
belief) is the real meaning of *faith*. How are we doing in moving
beyond feelings of worthlessness? Are we helping others to do
the same?

My own sin will not hinder the working of God's goodness.

— Julian of Norwich

WE ALL FAIL AND FALL SHORT, Julian is saying. We are capable of inappropriate choices and harmful behavior. But that does not slow down the work of God's goodness, which is far more powerful than our shortcomings. Goodness can and will triumph over our failures.

The fullness of joy is to behold God in everything.

— Julian of Norwich

LIKE SO MANY MYSTICS, Julian has come to a point where she can find God in everything. That is how deep her awareness of blessing or goodness lies. How are we doing? Can we find God in all things, even difficult things? Are we making some progress in doing so?

God is justice.... God wants to be known and loved
through Justice and Compassion now and forever.

— Julian of Norwich

A TEACHING found in Aquinas and Eckhart and elsewhere is
that God is justice. Where there is justice and people are working for justice, there God is. Compassion and justice go together because compassion is not just feeling sorry for people:
compassion is justice in action. It is our work to interfere with
injustice and to bring justice alive. Ask yourself: What work for
justice am I engaged in at this time?

"That which is impossible for you is not impossible to me: I will pre-serve my word in all things and I will make all things well." This is the great deed that Our Lord will do.... Our good Lord answered all my questions and doubts by saying with full energy: "I can make all things well, I know how to make all things well, I desire to make all things well, I will make all things well. And you will see with your own eyes that every kind of thing will be well."

— Julian of Norwich

GOD MAKES ALL THINGS WELL. God (for Julian, Christ is an-other name for God) is a healer. We are other Christs, other healers also, working to make all things well. Thanks to the power of God, all things can be healed and made well again, for God can do so, knows how to do so, desires to do so, and will do so. There is deep hope in this observation by Julian.

Wellness, wholeness, healing, and salvation are possible. Julian sings of the hope that comes with faith. Do we find that our faith heals our own cynicism and despair?

Our Lord Jesus oftentimes said: "This I am. This I am.
I am what you love. I am what you enjoy. I am what you serve.
I am what you long for. I am what you desire.
I am what you intend. I am all that is."

— Julian of Norwich

JULIAN IS TELLING US to pay attention to our deepest desires. Our desires point us to the end point, to Divinity itself,
the "alpha and omega." Is Julian's experience yours also, that
Christ or God is "what I love, what I enjoy, what I serve, what
I long for"? Is this an invitation to purify what we love, enjoy,
serve, and long for?

I saw a great oneing between Christ and us because when he was in pain we were in pain. All creatures of God's creation that can suffer pain suffered with him. The sky and the earth failed at the time of Christ's dying because he too was part of nature.

— Julian of Norwich

NOTICE HOW JULIAN DERIVES from Jesus' death that God too is far from invulnerable, in fact very vulnerable. God undergoes deaths and suffering also. And Jesus' cruel death on a cross was a cosmic event — it incorporated all the suffering of the creatures of nature. When you have a broken heart, a wrenching depth of pain, have you felt a "great oneing" with Christ?

It is God's will that we do all in our power to keep ourselves strong, for happiness is everlasting and pain is passing and will end. Therefore it is not God's will that we pine and mourn over feelings of pain but that we get better and continue to enjoy life.

— Julian of Norwich

HAPPINESS IS EVERLASTING and pain is temporary, Julian says. Happiness is more enduring than suffering. Suffering will someday cease. Is that your experience? She urges us to move beyond pining, mourning, and wallowing in our woes to become strong and get better in order to continue to enjoy life. The goal she presents is the enjoyment of life.

From suffering I have learned this:
That whoever is sore wounded by love will never be made whole
unless she embrace the very same love which wounded her.

— Mechtild of Magdeburg

THIS PARADOXICAL TEACHING from Mechtild is about loving our enemies, about embracing our wounds. It also reminds us that all our deepest wounds come from love itself. Betrayal, for example, only happens because love and trust existed in the first place. But her medicine is to embrace the love that wounds us. This is harder but more effective than being in denial, taking a pill, or burying our anger in bitterness, wouldn't you say?

There comes a time when both body and soul enter into such a vast darkness that one loses light and consciousness and knows nothing more of God's intimacy. At such a time when the light in the lantern burns out the beauty of the lantern can no longer be seen. With longing and distress we are reminded of our nothingness.

— Mechtild of Magdeburg

THREE HUNDRED YEARS before John of the Cross talked about the "dark night of the soul," Mechtild talks here about not only the light going out but the memory of the light and the lantern itself vanishing. Apparently the dark night is a universal phenomenon. Have you felt it? Are we feeling it as a species at this time in history? What does it have to teach us? Why are we being visited by the dark night?

At such a time I pray to God: "Lord, this burden is too heavy for me!" And God replies: "I will take this burden first and clasp it close to Myself and that way you may more easily bear it."

— Mechtild of Magdeburg

LIKE JULIAN, MECHTILD TEACHES that God undergoes the suffering and the loss and the dark night first. God clasps it close to the Godself. We therefore have some company in our brokenheartedness.

"I, God, am your playmate! I will lead the child in you in wonderful ways for I have chosen you. Beloved child, come swiftly to Me for I am truly in you. Remember this: The smallest soul of all is still the daughter of the Father, the sister of the Son, the friend of the Holy Spirit and the true bride of the Holy Trinity."

— Mechtild of Magdeburg

MECHTILD IS LISTENING to the voice of God. She tells us God wants to be known as a companion to children, to the *puer* or *puella* nature of our souls even as adults. Playfulness is encouraged. We are chosen to be playmates of the Divine. Since Sophia, or Wisdom, is always playing in the world (see Proverbs 8:30–31), Mechtild is inviting us into the realm of Wisdom.

"I who am Divine am truly in you. I can never be sundered from you; however far we be parted, never can we be separated. I am in you and you are in Me. We could not be any closer. We two are fused into one, poured into a single mould; thus unwearied, we shall remain forever."

— Mechtild of Magdeburg

GOD WITHIN, GOD TRULY WITHIN. God deeply within. God so surely within that nothing can separate us from God. Panentheism: "I in you and you are in Me." We cannot be any closer to God. We are fused into one, and this forever. Have you ever glimpsed the truth Mechtild has tasted and is teaching us? It is the same experience that Julian also spoke of — a true oneing, no separation, nothing between us and God.

The day of my spiritual awakening was the day I saw
and knew I saw all things in God and God in all things.

— Mechtild of Magdeburg

MECHTILD IS SPEAKING of her own evolution, her own spiritual growth. She was asleep, unawake, unaware until the day she woke up and underwent a spiritual awakening. And the test of her awakening? Panentheism. A deep awareness and a sure awareness — "I saw and knew I saw" — that all things are in God and God is in all things. Do you feel yourself moving from sleep and forgetfulness to an awakening? As was the case with Mechtild, is this awakening grounded in experiential panentheism — seeing God in all things and all things in God? Is this the meaning of enlightenment? Mechtild seems to think so. Meister Eckhart calls this breakthrough the realization that "I and God are one."

*The truly wise person kneels at the feet of all creatures
and is not afraid to endure the mockery of others.*

— Mechtild of Magdeburg

AUTHENTIC WISDOM — to see God in all things — carries with it a sense of humility and reverence. The idea that reverence and humility are shown by "lowering" ourselves is rooted in our language: *Humility* comes from the Latin word for "earth," which is *humus*. Meanwhile, to genuflect is to bend the knee in reverence and respect (*genou* is the word for "knee" in French). Kneeling brings us closer to the earth, down into our lower chakras, and more literally eye-to-eye with all creatures. This signifies an I-thou attitude: a relationship coming more from our hearts and less from our heads. Reverence does not come from the head.

Maybe our ecological crises today are the result of our failure to show reverence to all creatures, to kneel at their feet, and in doing so invite the mockery of an anthropocentric, human-centered, rationalistic mindset and economic system that rewards those "above" and exploits or ignores those "below."

Fish cannot drown in the water, birds cannot sink in the air,
gold cannot perish in the refiner's fire.
This God gives to all creatures: To develop and seek
their own nature — how then can I withstand mine?

— Mechtild of Magdeburg

MECHTILD POSES what seems to be a human dilemma: Do fish and birds ever question the elements they were born into? Fish will never breathe air, nor birds water, yet humans often seem to mistrust and "withstand" their true natures. Why is that, and what is your own nature? Are you made to swim like a fish, soar like a bird, burn like gold in a refiner's fire? Think, dance, create, exercise compassion? Are you developing your nature or resisting it?

How does God come to us? Like dew on the flowers.
Like the song of the birds! Yes, God gives the Godself
with all creatures wholly to me.

— Mechtild of Magdeburg

DO WE EXPECT GOD TO APPEAR as a white-robed patriarch with a booming voice or like "dew on the flowers" or the song of a bird? Like all mystics, Jesus included, Mechtild presents mystical experiences in nature as the primary avenue for connecting with the Divine. In Mechtild's experience, God gives himself with all creatures wholly to you. Have you ever felt so immersed in connection with nature that every part of you felt touched?

yes! Grammy

Love flows from God to humans without effort:
As a bird glides through the air without moving its wings —
thus they go wherever they wish united in body and soul
yet separate in form.

— Mechtild of Magdeburg

MECHTILD SUGGESTS that the subtle presence of divine love, the movement of grace, is a simple flowing, coasting like a gliding bird, a gentle movement without effort. It involves not a laborious climb, an ascetic-driven march, but a kind of gliding. Gliding is defined by silence, stillness everywhere. Have you experienced what Mechtild describes? When? How did it change you? Did it deepen your trust?

From the very beginning God loved us.
The Holy Trinity gave itself in the creation of all things
and made us, body and soul, in infinite love.
We were fashioned most nobly.

— Mechtild of Magdeburg

IN THE TRADITION of original blessing instead of original sin, Mechtild declares that we were "fashioned most nobly" and "from the very beginning God loved us." We were born in infinite love. This includes our parents (whatever we may perceive their shortcomings to be), as well as the air, the flowers, all creatures, the earth, the stars, the eons — all of it was a fashioning most holy, washed in infinite love.

Divinity sings this song to our souls: "O lovely rose on the thorn!
O hovering bee in the honey! O pure dove in your being!
O glorious sun in your setting! O full moon in your course!
From you I, your God, will never turn away."

— Mechtild of Magdeburg

WE OFTEN READ OR SING the psalms, and we are encouraged to praise God with our songs. Here Mechtild turns the tables. God is praising and singing and presenting the psalmody to us. That's a nice change, isn't it? Have you ever heard Divinity singing to your soul? What did, or might, it sound like?

God you are the sun; I am your reflection.
When God shines we must reflect.

— Mechtild of Magdeburg

Is this another way to say we are made in the image of God? Notice Mechtild's use of "must." This is not a moral must, a duty, an obligation, or a commandment. It is an organic must, a natural must. A kind of fate or destiny. We cannot help but reflect the beautiful sun. Have you had this experience, in which you felt God shining and were compelled to respond and reflect that light?

> *I ponder much and reflect in my human sense*
> *how wonderful my soul is!*
>
> — Mechtild of Magdeburg

HOW OFTEN DO YOU PONDER the wondrous nature of your soul? How it gives life and meaning to your senses? Do you stop once a month, once a week, once an hour to appreciate your inner self — the joy and beauty, the wonder and delight, the thoughts and dreams that go on inside of you? Can you remember the last time you did this? If not, take a break from whatever distracts you — television, work, compulsive habits — and do so. It is time well spent.

The very sight of God causes delight.
At the sight of God the mind can do nothing but delight.

— Thomas Aquinas

LIKE MECHTILD, THOMAS AQUINAS SPEAKS of the mind undergoing the "must" of delight. For Aquinas in the thirteenth century, "mind" was much more than the "thinking brain" of Descartes and modern European thinkers. The mind included the imagination and memory, the capacity for wonder and for birthing creativity. In the presence of God, Aquinas says, humans don't suddenly "know"; they delight. All doubt, skepticism, and even thinking give way to overwhelming delight. Is it important that our understanding of human consciousness include delight at its base? Can we give delight if we have not tasted it first? Can we taste it if we don't praise it as a goal and a value?

Joy is a human being's noblest act.

— Thomas Aquinas

THIS IS AN EARTH-SHATTERING STATEMENT. It turns the past four hundred years of western European thinking upside down. Aquinas, one of the greatest geniuses who ever lived, does not declare that rationality is our noblest act; joy is. Joy is the beginning and the end of all we do; it is the best we do.

If Aquinas is correct, we can ask: Is our educational system operating from joy? Our media? Our politics? Our economics? Our religions? Our worship? If not, how do we change, so that joy and nobility guide our souls and society again? How do we keep alive our nobility as a species?

All things love God. All things are united
according to friendship to each other and to God.

— Thomas Aquinas

GIVEN THE STATE OF THE WORLD, it would seem this is a naive teaching — that all things love one another — from a brilliant but naive premodern thinker. Or is this the mystic's way of recognizing what science today calls the interconnection of all things? If all things are interconnected, isn't there a wisdom in seeing all things as friends? Isn't friendship about interconnectivity?

Can we take today's science and bathe it in the graceful waters of mystical awareness to get at its deepest meanings? Aquinas may be teaching us the meaning of what today's science is rediscovering.

God is most joyful and is therefore supremely conscious.

— Thomas Aquinas

WE HEAR A LOT ABOUT CONSCIOUSNESS today, but does anyone connect consciousness and joy? For Aquinas, joy is not just our noblest act but a birthplace of consciousness. Because God is most joyful, God is most conscious. The same would clearly hold for us: the more joy we tap into, the greater our consciousness. Can we, when we want more self-awareness and conscious understanding, reach for joy? Can we birth a culture that puts joy first?

God delights. God is always rejoicing and doing so
with a single and simple delight. In fact, it is appropriate to say
that love and joy are the only human emotions
that we can attribute literally to God.

— Thomas Aquinas

AQUINAS ELEVATES LOVE and joy as the only human emotions directly connected to God. Not revenge. Not anger. Not sorrow. Not regret. Not desire. How does this correspond with your image of God or Divinity or the Creator? Do you see God "always rejoicing" with a "single and simple delight"? Do you practice rejoicing with a single and simple delight? Do you seek out God to rejoice with the Divinity? Does our culture?

Every love makes the beloved to be in the lover, and the lover in the beloved. The lover is not satisfied with a superficial apprehension of the beloved, but strives to gain an intimate knowledge of everything pertinent to the beloved, so as to penetrate into the very soul.

— Thomas Aquinas

IT IS PERHAPS SURPRISING to read a medieval mystic and theologian write in such profound and erotic language about love. True lovers strive for a mutual "in-ness," so that lover merges with beloved, beloved with lover. Love drives us beyond superficial knowledge of the beloved to an intimate, in-depth knowledge, a penetration to the very soul of the beloved. Have you had such a sensual-spiritual experience of love?

Four proximate effects may be ascribed to love:
namely, melting, enjoyment, languor and fervor.

— Thomas Aquinas

AQUINAS IS SAYING that the first effect of love is melting. Do you find that coldness, distance, indifference — all are melted by the experience of love? Next comes enjoyment. Joy follows from love, mutual enjoyment between lover and beloved. Next comes languor, a desire for one's beloved when the lover is absent. How real is that, how deep is one's languor? And finally comes fervor. Zeal, fire, energy are all aroused by love. It appears love truly takes us to our soul-depths, where melting, joy, languor, and fervor are born and nurtured.

The freezing or hardening of the heart is a disposition incompatible with love, while melting denotes a softening of the heart, whereby the heart shows itself to be ready for the entrance of the beloved. If, then, the beloved is present and possessed, pleasure or enjoyment ensues.

— Thomas Aquinas

AQUINAS IS SPEAKING of the melting effect of love, the "softening of the heart," that opens us to others. No love can follow without this softening, and it applies to every relationship, romantic, filial, and divine. In our time, has patriarchy been good at teaching men how to soften their hearts? Might a great deal of melting be in store? Aquinas promises that enjoyment and pleasure ensue when the heart is ready for the beloved to enter. But that only happens when melting occurs. Hardness of heart is incompatible with love.

But if the beloved is absent, two passions arise: namely, sadness at its absence, which is denoted by languor; and an intense desire to possess the beloved, which is signified by fervor.

— Thomas Aquinas

ABSENCE AROUSES SADNESS and a yearning to possess. Thus languor and fervor are triggered by love. These sound like very powerful forces, powerful energies. How adept are we at tapping into them, using them as our fuel, our fire? Look for sadness and a yearning to possess, for languor and fervor in your own soul. Look for the fire and the zeal. Good things can come of reconnecting to these deep feelings. When we lose this sense of fervor or zeal we become couch potatoes or we fall into depression; we can easily turn to addictions to fill the void in our souls.

Love is cause of all that the lover does....
Love is the cause of both pleasure and sorrow.

— Thomas Aquinas

DO YOU AGREE WITH THIS? Does love so take us over that it becomes a cause of everything we do? How great is that? What are the dangers in this? Are you and I lovers in all we do? Lovers of whom? For whom? Whom are we serving? How does our work derive energy and fire from this love, and who else is benefiting? Can we do better purifying our love and purifying our work? This teaching is about bringing eros to everything we do, for eros is the passion for living that Aquinas celebrates.

Looking deeply at sorrow, Aquinas has learned that even sorrow happens because of love. The deepest loss is directly related to our deepest love, to what has given us great joy. Thus it is love that undergirds all our deepest experiences in life, the negative as well as the positive. Love causes pleasure and love causes sorrow. Love is the common thread of all life's adventures.

While pleasure can be entire and perfect,
sadness is always partial.

— Thomas Aquinas

WOW! AGAIN, TO MODERN EARS, Aquinas sounds almost naive, proposing that only pleasure can be "entire and perfect," while depression is temporary. What would he make of our modern world, so steeped in cynicism, moroseness, and clinical depression? Aquinas lived at a time when people believed goodness and pleasure were more foundational than sadness and woe. Does any Western culture or religion still teach that? But is this not what indigenous peoples demonstrate? I once met a man who was living among indigenous people on an island in the Amazon rain forest. I asked him what they teach him: "Joy," he said. "They experience more joy in a day than I do in a year."

Hope is about the possible; despair is about the impossible.

— Thomas Aquinas

WE DESPAIR WHEN WE SEE NO WAY OUT. Suicide is a yielding to this feeling that there is no way out, to despair. Young people who can see no way out of some oppressive circumstance are often driven to violence and may end up in prison for this reason. Despair is real and very dark. We humans are very adept at seeing the impossible and dwelling on it until it takes over our souls.

Those who maintain hope are always looking for possibilities, for angles, for creative solutions, for alternatives. Hope keeps their souls and imaginations alive and, above all, creative. Artists know this. This is their vocation, to tell the truth but always within the context of the possible.

No person is in such darkness
as to be completely devoid of divine light.
The divine light shines in the darkness and radiates upon all.

— Thomas Aquinas

AQUINAS IS TEACHING that we cannot escape the light. Even in the darkest of circumstances, the darkest of the dark nights, the divine light shines and radiates therein. Even when we cannot see it. This takes some hard believing, some deep trusting. How are we doing? Can we believe in the light even in the pitch darkness? Can we bring it alive for others? How?

Every love causes ecstasy.
To suffer ecstasy means to be placed outside oneself.

— Thomas Aquinas

AQUINAS SAYS WE "SUFFER" ECSTASY; we undergo it. Ecstasy is bigger than us and that is why it affects us so deeply. It transforms us and makes us new. It makes us alive when we are feeling deadened and puts us outside ourselves, beyond our pains and woes and doubts. Where do we find such ecstasy? It comes with every love. A shocking observation! The love of a tree, of a poem, of a flower, of a bird, of a dance, of music, of strangers, of lovers, of relatives, of enemies — any love whatsoever causes ecstasy. So ecstasy is not rare, it is not rationed, it is everywhere love is. Wow! No wonder Aquinas put optimism ahead of pessimism. He found love and ecstasy everywhere. Despite the cynicism and rapaciousness of today's society, can you see the abundance of ecstasy in every love?

In the Song of Songs (chapter 5) we read: "My beloved, you are drunk with love." Those who are drunk are not inside of themselves but outside of themselves. Those who are filled with spiritual gifts, all their intention is carried toward God....Just as those who hold their mouth to a fountain of wine are drunk so those who hold their mouth, that is their desire, at the foundation of life and sweetness are drunk. And so they are drunk, since "with you there is a fountain of life."

— Thomas Aquinas

AQUINAS IS ENDORSING DRUNKENNESS here. Time to get high. Time to get outside ourselves. Time for some ecstasy. This is what mystics do and what mystics teach. Not just any drunkenness, but to be "drunk with love," which brings on ecstasy. When were you last inebriated with love? What did it do for you? What did it do for others? When did you last hold your mouth, that is your desire, at the foundation of life and sweetness and get drunk? It sounds like fun, getting drunk on the fountain of life. Time for an encore?

*Love brings it about that lovers are directed
not only toward themselves, but also toward others.*

— Thomas Aquinas

REAL LOVE LEADS BEYOND THE LOVERS to others. Love expands. Love is inclusive. It enlarges the soul; it enlarges one's actions, one's politics, one's economics, one's thoughts. Love is not self-serving or exclusive. It expands consciousness and births imagination, it struggles for justice, it stands in solidarity, it dares, it fights, it blossoms into compassion. Can you find new ways to shine your love outward?

God puts into creatures, along with a kind of "sheen," a reflection of God's own luminous "ray," which is "the fountain of all light." Shining reflections of the divine radiance must be understood as the sharing of God's likeness and constitute those "beautifying" reflections that make beauty in things.

— Thomas Aquinas

AQUINAS, LIKE SO MANY OTHER MYSTICS, sees the light of God in all things. Not a dull light but a sheen, a luminous ray. While it is a reflection of God, the "fountain of all light," this divine radiance shines from within and is the source of beauty. We are ourselves shining reflections of the radiance. Can you believe that? Try meditating on that. Do you see any and all beauty as divine radiance? Does such a perspective change what you see? Can you share it with others? What journey does it take you on?

*God is supersubstantial beauty and God bestows
beauty on all created beings.*

— Thomas Aquinas

I AM NOT SURE exactly what "supersubstantial beauty" is or looks like, but it sounds very great and beyond words. It is so much beauty that it transcends our perception. That's what God is according to Aquinas. Then, God bestows beauty on all beings, which means that God certainly must have a different standard of beauty than Hollywood. Can you imagine God as supersubstantial beauty? Does your religion proclaim or pro-·mote this idea? Could you spend a day seeing this beauty in every person and creature you meet? How does this alter your understanding of beauty?

The highest beauty is in the Godhead,
since beauty consists in comeliness:
but God is beauty itself, beautifying all things.

— Thomas Aquinas

VERY FEW PREACHERS and very few theologians in the past three hundred years have spoken of God as beauty. This is an important ethical and spiritual category, and it has been missing from modern consciousness. Descartes, the father still (alas!) of modern Western education, developed an entire philosophy but with no philosophy of beauty or aesthetics. This is one reason for our global ecological crisis: Beauty has no ethical or philosophical standing in the modern era. We can bring it back. We must. Time is running out for humans, and nothing motivates us like beauty. Beauty gets us out of our couchpotatoitis. Out of our couches! To defend the earth and her beauty. Gaia is beauty itself, beautifying all things.

By dwelling on creatures the mind is inflated
to love the divine goodness. We love God and know God
in the mirror of God's creatures.

— Thomas Aquinas

MIRROR MYSTICISM IS SEEING every creature as an image or mirror of Divinity. Every creature reveals something about God to us — maybe it is beauty; maybe humor that shines through; maybe simplicity; maybe complexity. With the right eyes of perception, everything reveals something of the Divine to us. We meditate on creatures to taste the "divine goodness," or blessing. We do not have to choose between God and the world, or turn from the world to find God, for "we love God and know God in the mirror of God's creatures." Can you learn to do this a little more each day?

God is supremely good and therefore supremely generous.
Sheer joy is God's and this demands companionship.

— Thomas Aquinas

GOD'S GOODNESS IS NOT LIMITED. It is supreme. It is also generous, indeed, supremely generous. Generosity is a divine attribute. For us to develop our generosity is for us to develop our God-likeness.

Moreover, the sheer joy of God is the very cause of the universe, since joy demands companionship. Joy seeks to be shared. There lie Aquinas's thoughts on why the universe exists — for the sake of joy. To share joy, God created others, an enlarged community. Community is nothing if it is not a place/space of shared joy.

Self-love is the form and root of all friendship. Well-ordered self-love is right and natural — so much so that the person who hates himself or herself sins against nature. To know and to appreciate your own worth is no sin.

— Thomas Aquinas

SOME RELIGIOUS TEACHERS BUILD THEIR THEOLOGIES around the central idea "What a wretch am I." Hating oneself, subscribing to a self-hating theology, is not Aquinas's teaching, and it is not healthy psychology either. Authentic self-love is the very basis of friendship — how can we love others well if we have not learned to love ourselves well?

Aquinas goes further: Self-hatred, he says, is a sin against nature. That is strong language. But consider this self-love in the context of the rest of nature — does any tree or whale, horse or eagle, blade of grass or star hate itself? No. As Mechtild says, they seek only to fulfill their true natures, to do the work of being the best possible tree, whale, horse, eagle, and so on. It is false and pseudo-humility to hate oneself. We need to come to know ourselves and appreciate our own worth and to help others to do the same. There lies authentic friendship.

All things together are very good by reason of the order of the universe, which is the ultimate and noblest perfection in things.

— Thomas Aquinas

AQUINAS PUTS OUR EXISTENCE and that of all things in the context of the entire universe. His is not a psychologically based spirituality but a cosmologically based spirituality. If we are looking to find the "ultimate and noblest perfection in things," he proposes, then look to the whole. Today, we know the order of the universe is a very dynamic order, a rapidly evolving order, an order in motion, an order of the birth, death, and resurrection of galaxies, supernovas, stars, and planets, including earth. We all exist to serve a larger order, the cosmos itself.

One meditates on creation in order to view and marvel at divine wisdom. Each creature is made as a witness to God insofar as each creature is a witness to God's power and omnipotence; and its beauty is a witness to the divine wisdom.

— Thomas Aquinas

THINK OF EVERY CREATURE as a "witness to God," a testimony that wisdom exists, that beauty exists, that it is constantly incarnated and made flesh in so many forms and so many eras and evolutionary epochs. A never-ending caravan of history and species and individuals — all bearing witness to divine wisdom unfolding within and about us. Apply this observation about meditating on creation to the work of the scientist. Aquinas exalts the vocation of science.

This is what the philosopher and the poet share in common: both are concerned with the marvelous. Amazement is the beginning of philosophy. Wonder is a kind of desire in knowing. It is the cause of delight because it carries with it the hope of discovery.

— Thomas Aquinas

THERE IS DELIGHT IN KNOWING and thus a strong desire to know. Our yearning to know bears with it a hope of excitement — the excitement of discovery. Learning is therefore an adventure. And where does it all begin? With awe, amazement, wonder, and a touch of the marvelous. Look for the marvelous. Expect it.

The idea that the philosopher and the poet share common ground of wonder is not a modern idea — it is a premodern teaching. The modern idea, such as Descartes taught, is that philosophy begins with doubt. How different is doubt from wonder? Education is still built on Descartes's ideas of doubt and not on the premodern idea of wonder. Such education can only lead to knowledge; it will never lead to wisdom. Awe is the beginning of wisdom. Maybe it is time to change education so that it can excite learning and wisdom again.

*There can be no question that to study creatures
is to build up one's Christian faith.*

— Thomas Aquinas

SOME PEOPLE BELIEVE FAITH comes from studying the Bible exclusively. Aquinas goes much further. The time we spend learning about nature is time spent developing our awareness of Christ. Isn't Christ the light in all things? All of nature is a "book about God," as Eckhart put it. Thus to be a scientist and to be one who studies nature is to learn about the Divine. Loving nature, studying and observing it, perhaps by growing a garden, befriending an animal, watching the stars, or studying the human body — all these are avenues to deeper faith development. Science is a sacred act. Study is a yoga, a spiritual practice.

God is in all things as giving them being, power, and operation.
One can say that God is more closely united
to each thing than the thing is to itself.

— Thomas Aquinas

NOT ONLY IS GOD WITHIN ALL THINGS but God is intimately within all things, the active power within all things — giving them their being and existence, their unique operation. Experiencing this realization takes practice and meditation. A good place to begin is to meditate alone in nature or with a close friend: How do I perceive God as being, as bestower of power and of operation? Do I sense that at these deep levels I/we are not alone but are part of a far broader and deeper river of history? Part of an ocean of evolution far greater than ourselves? Part of a dynamic and evolving community of beings?

Divine life is per se alive since it is not vivifying as some other things in God. It is supereminently alive ... and ineffable.... Divine life is praised above all life because of its fecundity, by which it produces all lives. It is most generous because it is not narrowed toward one kind of life but has a comprehensive fullness of all life.

— Thomas Aquinas

DIVINE LIFE IS ABOVE ALL LIVING, animated, alive. It is "per se alive." Divine life is also preeminently fertile and creative. It is the creativity behind all creativity. It is the source of all life and for this reason it is supremely generous — not narrow and stingy. Clearly, it invites us to be the same — not narrow, not possessing, not stingy, but giving and giving generously. Are we this way also? Do we live for life's sake? Do we taste aliveness in all its depths and all its variety and all its preciousness? Do we allow ourselves the time to sink into life and to taste this deep fullness? Or do we take life for granted? Do we take journeys into life itself to praise life and to thank life and to live the privilege of our limited days more fully? Do we refuse to take life for granted? Let us practice this great refusal.

God has produced a work in which the divine likeness
is clearly reflected — I mean by this, the world itself.
God's love is not about a private conversation;
it goes out universally to all the divine works.

— Thomas Aquinas

DESPITE OUR INTIMATE CONNECTION to the Divine, our relationship is not a "private conversation." It is the world itself — not any individual in it — that is the clearest expression of the image of God or the reflection of the Divine. God's love is outgoing and extends to the entire universe, "to all the divine works." Is our love growing this way also? Do we imbibe and fall in love with the entire universe and understand that to be our prayer and our relationship to God? Aquinas challenges us to move from psychology to cosmology. God's love extends to all beings, not just to humans and certainly not just to humans of a particular tribe or religion or history.

All artists love what they give birth to — parents love their children; poets love their poems; craftspeople love their handiwork. How then could God hate a single thing since God is the artist of everything?... God is an artist and the universe is God's work of art. All natural things are produced by divine art and can rightly be called God's works of art.

— Thomas Aquinas

IF THE UNIVERSE IS GOD'S WORK OF ART, then every natural thing, every creature, yourself included, is "God's work of art." Does that add to or take away from your sense of self, from your sense of the world? Think about the things you have made in your life — do you agree with Aquinas that artists love what they give birth to? What are you giving birth to in your work, in your citizenship, in your community, in your family? Do you do so with love?

How does that affect your understanding of God — to imagine God as the artist of everything? Is it possible to imagine that such a God would love every single thing? Does religion teach this?

God's spirit is said to move over the waters as the will of artists
moves over the material to be shaped by their art.

— Thomas Aquinas

THIS OBSERVATION IS A GREAT AFFIRMATION of the work of the artist. The same spirit — Aquinas is saying — that launched creation itself infuses the work and mind of the artist. The artist is a channel for the Holy Spirit at work. What has been your experience with art? Do you feel moved spiritually by music, literature, movies, dance, poetry, architecture? Do you engage in these practices? What about everyday expressions of art, such as the art of raising your children or the art of decorating a room, the art of conversation, the art of growing a garden or cooking a meal? Do you recognize the Spirit at work in your many experiences of art?

One of the functions of divine wisdom is to create.
God's wisdom is that of artists, whose knowledge
of what they make is practical as well as theoretical.

— Thomas Aquinas

WISDOM IS CREATIVE. Hildegard of Bingen said, "There is wisdom in all created works." Here Aquinas compares God to artists, since both don't just contemplate creation in the abstract but make things and accomplish things. Form breaks into multiple expressions. A society that cares about wisdom cares about creativity.

God is the Source who has no Source.

— Thomas Aquinas

THERE ARE MANY "DEFINITIONS" of Divinity, but this is a particularly striking one. It is very feminist, for women philosophers love to talk about the "Source." God stands out as a Source without a Source. That is a great mystery, for everything we experience in nature has a source, a cause — we trace rivers to their source. We trace weather systems to their source. We trace mountains to that moment in geological time when they were born. Can we rest in the Source of all other sources and derive our own creative powers there? Renew our own sourcehood, so to speak?

The word "Lord" means the maker of all creation as in Judith 16:
"All your creation serves you."

— Thomas Aquinas

MANY PEOPLE USE THE WORD *LORD* in their prayers and also in their projections. Here Aquinas teaches us that the primary meaning of *Lord* is "the maker of all creation." God the Creator is what the word *Lord* refers to. To love that Lord we must love creation, study it, listen to those who do the same. Otherwise we are trapped in projection alone. Instead of worshipping God, we are worshipping our own ego, the birthplace of our projections. To worship one's projections is plain and simple idolatry. Individuals and also religious institutions and traditions need to be on guard against idolatry. Jesus warned: "Not all who say 'Lord, Lord' will enter the kingdom of heaven."

Sacred writings are bound in two volumes — that of creation and that of the Holy Scriptures.... Visible creatures are like a book in which we read the knowledge of God. One has every right to call God's creatures God's "works," for they express the divine mind just as effects manifest their cause. "The works of the Lord are the words of the Lord" (Eccles. 42.15).

— Thomas Aquinas

ONCE AGAIN AQUINAS, a premodern thinker, is more sophisticated than some modern thinkers, who confuse the word of God with literal words in a book (even a holy book such as the Bible). Premodern times were not illiterate times; the Bible was read and revered. Yet the word of God was considered, above all, creation itself. Thus to study the word of God is to study nature. Scientists have as much to teach us about God as do biblical scholars.

To talk about Christ as the Logos, or word of God, is also to talk about Christ as the Cosmic Christ, the image of God present in every creature in the universe. Nature is as much a sacred book as the Bible. Will we ever recover this balanced and fuller understanding of where revelation is to be found? If we do, will respecting the sacredness of nature usher in a truly ecological era? Or will humans continue to use one holy book to justify destroying God's earthly one?

When Thomas Aquinas defined the transcendence of grace by invoking the Aristotelian idea of nature, he was not merely making a reasoned option in favor of the Philosopher. Rather he was giving supreme expression to that Christianity in which a return to the gospel had secured for the believer a presence in the world, for the theologian a mature awareness of nature, and for the apostle an effective appreciation of man [humanity]. . . . History shows that it was the Christian's return to the gospel which guaranteed his presence in the world and that it was this presence in the world which secured the efficacy of the gospel.

— M. D. Chenu

CHENU, INSTEAD OF PITTING WORLD against church or faith against secular society, instructs us that, as in the great reformation and renaissance period of the twelfth century, a return to gospel values assures for the believer a secure place as "a presence in the world" and for the thinker "a mature awareness of nature." This necessarily includes a deep appreciation for science, since it is science's task to teach us about nature, and for the preacher, who provides an appreciation of human nature. Do these results still hold today? Are they key to moving beyond cultural wars and to integrating faith and culture, so that one nourishes the other instead of one beating up on the other?

Good is more powerful than evil. As long as we are living,
we can never be so stuck in evil that divine grace cannot get us out.

— Thomas Aquinas

IT IS GOOD TO REMIND OURSELVES that evil does not have
the last word, that goodness is more powerful and more omnipresent than evil. It does not always appear that way. Sometimes evil seems to take over and triumph. As Rabbi Zalman
Schachter-Shalomi says: "There is more good than evil in the
world but not by much." There is something realistic in this as-
sessment. Yet, as Aquinas insists, divine grace can always extri-
cate us from evil. Evil does not and must not have the last word.

The first requirement, then, for the contemplation of wisdom is that we should take complete possession of our minds before anything else does, so that we can fill the whole house with the contemplation of wisdom. It is also necessary that we be fully present there, concentrating in such a way that our aim is not diverted to other matters.

— Thomas Aquinas

HERE AQUINAS TEACHES US about meditation. It begins with taking "complete possession" of our minds — taking them back from the distractions and busyness of the monkey mind that wants to chatter and constantly make things happen inside itself. Why do this? "So that we can fill the whole house with the contemplation of wisdom." Our mind is a house, and we must actively court wisdom, let wisdom take it over. To do so, we must be fully present there. Let go of distractions and diversions, focus on the present moment, don't wander into busy thoughts and projections. Concentrate.

This ancient teaching about meditation is well-known in the East, but it is good to see it taught in the Western tradition as well.

It says in Wisdom 8.16: "I will enter my house and find rest with her," namely with wisdom. When our interior house is entirely emptied and we are fully present there in our intention, the text tells us what to do next: "And play there." There are two features of play that make it appropriate to compare the contemplation of wisdom to playing. First, we enjoy playing, and there is the greatest enjoyment of all to be had in the contemplation of wisdom. Second, playing has no purpose beyond itself; what we do in play is done for its own sake. And the same applies to the pleasure of wisdom.

— Thomas Aquinas

MEDITATION, CONTEMPLATION OF THE DIVINE, is often approached solemnly, yet Aquinas emphasizes the pleasure in wisdom. If through meditation we empty our house, our mind, of cluttered thoughts, wisdom always shows up, ready to play. She "plays with God before the creation of the world" (Proverbs 8:30–31). In other words, what comes after the hard work of concentration? Play! Contemplation is a lot like play because it is enjoyable and "has no purpose beyond itself," or as Eckhart taught, "without a why." Deep prayer is not about getting or acquiring something. It is about doing something without a why, for no purpose at all but the act itself. Therefore it is about deepening our being.

The effects of love should be displayed as well as felt.

— Thomas Aquinas

TRUE LOVE PRODUCES SOMETHING, displays its existence. Love is felt but feeling is not enough. Love is to be put into action. Maybe this is why American philosopher William Hocking said, "The prophet is the mystic in action." True mysticism leads to healthy action. True tasting of nonaction leads to authentic action.

Nonaction is a kind of action. Omission is directly opposed to justice...because it is non-fulfillment of a good of virtue but only under the aspect of what is due, which pertains to justice.

— Thomas Aquinas

NOT TO ACT IS SOMETIMES MORE DANGEROUS and more grievous a mistake than to take the wrong action. There are numerous examples from history that support this observation by Aquinas. Are there examples from your own life that relate to this insight? Do you speak when virtue requires a voice in the name of justice?

An evil person can do ten thousand times more harm than a beast,
because we can use our reason to devise many diverse evils.

— Thomas Aquinas

AQUINAS HERE UNDERSCORES the power of the human mind
— our intellect and imagination together make us capable of
far more evil than the wildest beasts. Consider nuclear bombs.
Whales have been on the planet 56 million years longer than
humans, and yet they have not created anything resembling
such a horrible device. Why not? What does that tell us about
whales? About humans?

It is amazing that Aquinas spoke these words seven hundred years before Hitler or Stalin or Pol Pot. Yet Aquinas understood that the human capacity for evil is directly related to
our creativity and our imagination. Modern consciousness often
belittles creativity. We rarely teach it in modern education. Yet
our creativity is both our greatest strength and our most dangerous one. It is time to rediscover and take more seriously the
power of our creativity, a power for good and a power for destruction.

It is not from weakness that God has shared the government of the universe with creatures, but from an abundance of divine goodness have creatures been endowed with the dignity of causality. Every creature strives, by its activity, to communicate its own perfect being, in its own fashion to another; and in this it tends toward an imitation of the divine causality.

— Thomas Aquinas

THE UNIVERSE ITSELF IS GOVERNED by all creatures — the habits of evolution are intrinsic to creatures, and Divinity has endowed all creatures with "the dignity of causality." Think about it: a blade of grass produces another blade of grass; a mountain lion produces another mountain lion; a supernova explodes and gives birth to stars, which give birth to planets. And, of course, we humans express the dignity of causality on many fronts. Where does all this creativity come from? "From an abundance of divine goodness." This is blessing, original blessing, the sharing of the dignity of causality with so many species.

Do you agree that every creature is busy striving to communicate its own perfect being with others? In what ways are you part of this striving?

The intellect is the form of forms, because it has a form
that is not determined to one thing alone,
as is the case with a stone, but has a capacity for all forms.

— Thomas Aquinas

OUR MINDS, OUR AMAZING INTELLECTS, have something infinite about them. We are not limited to any single form but rather possess "a capacity for all forms." Where do they stop, our human musings and dreams and possibilities? Nowhere. Never. With no form, according to Aquinas. Even nothingness is part of our repertoire. Our minds are the "form of forms," both formless and beyond form. No wonder we are so dangerous! No wonder life is such an adventure. How often do you tap into these pools of infinity? What takes you there? What transformations happen?

The beauty of the artwork proceeds from the beauty of the artist.
When one thing makes and another is made,
the making stands between them.

— Thomas Aquinas

ART DOES NOT COME FROM NO PLACE. It comes from the artist. In some way, therefore, the beauty of the artist is present in the art; the beauty of the art reflects the beauty of the artist. Furthermore, this profound relationship between the maker and the thing made — the process that stands between them and connects them — is like another being that's been born, the relationship itself, the making.

When you consider the making of the things you've created, does a third thing, namely the making, stand between you? Do you honor that new relationship? If so, how do you do that?

Although a created being tends to the divine likeness in many ways, this one whereby it seeks the divine likeness by being the cause of others takes the ultimate place. We are God's co-workers.

— Thomas Aquinas

THE ULTIMATE EXPRESSION of the divine likeness in us is our capacity for causing others. Maybe this is why the works we give birth to — our children and our grandchildren, but also our books and our rituals, our buildings and our businesses, our ships and our airplanes, our pyramids and our work for social justice — all outlive us. As the cause of others, we live far beyond our years. Hopefully, we cause others some joy and some meaning long after we are gone and our personal acquaintance-ship has expired.

It is a great thing to do miracles,
but it is a greater thing to live virtuously.

— Thomas Aquinas

SOME PEOPLE LONG FOR and put their faith in miracles, which they define as sudden cures or dynamic healings, happenings that seem to defy nature's processes. They like to build their religious beliefs around such events. Aquinas was not one of these people. He believed that to live virtuously is the greatest miracle of all. The word *miracle* comes from the Latin word for "to wonder." But what is truly wondrous and amazing is to live a life of justice, of compassion, of integrity — or to strive to do so. Are we creating such a miracle? Is our culture?

A praiseworthy person is angry about the right things, at the right people, and in due moderation, since they are angry as they should be, when they should be and as long as they should be.

— Thomas Aquinas

MANY CHRISTIANS (and others) go through life in a passive-aggressive mode, holding their anger in because they are taught that anger is the work of the devil or at least a capital sin. Aquinas does not teach this. He believes anger has its place. He says that "nothing great happens without anger." Anger is a source of strength and perseverance. It keeps us going through rough times. The key is that we not let anger run our lives, that we find proper outlets for it that are nonviolent, that we let it go in due time, and that the right things get us angry — such as injustice.

People who are bitter retain their anger for a long time.

— Thomas Aquinas

DO YOU KNOW PEOPLE running on bitterness? Do you house some bitterness yourself? Life gives us plenty of reasons to be bitter, but in this observation Aquinas gets to the heart of bitterness so that we can be freed of it. The heart of bitterness comes from sitting on our anger, he proposes, and sitting on it for a long time. Healthy outlets for anger will cleanse us of our bitterness. Finding creative outlets for our anger helps in this process. But we must acknowledge our anger and respect it if we are to let it go.

*Those who are in great fear are so intent on their own passion
that they pay no attention to the suffering of others.*

— Thomas Aquinas

FEAR IS A GREAT PASSION. It can take over our souls. That is
why Aquinas warns us that to build our lives on fear is to ban-
ish compassion. Our fear can swallow our care of others. It runs
our lives, and it ruins our potential for making community,
building friendship, and exercising love. If fear is the opposite
of love, it is also the slayer of love and compassion. Beware of
fear. Develop a prayer life that stands up to fear and keeps fear
outside the door of our hearts.

Nothing should be feared — not human beings
and not any other thing....Perfect love drives out servile fear,
which is fear that expects punishment before everything else....
Christ had no servile fear.

— Thomas Aquinas

PSYCHOLOGIST JERRY JAMPOLSKY teaches that fear is the opposite of love. John's epistle says that "fear is driven out by perfect love" (1 John 4:18), and Aquinas offers a similar teaching, urging people to live without fear. And this includes religious people. Living our lives without fear is living a Christ-like life. If fear is the opposite of love and Christ taught love, then clearly a life of fear is not a Christ-like life.

How much does fear play a role in our lives, individually or collectively? Do our religions preach a servile fear of God? Is that not the opposite of preaching love? Do politicians and the media exploit fear? Is that not the opposite of building community?

Courage, having a heart that recognizes fear but does not allow it to take over one's soul, is one of the surest signs of a truly spiritual person.

Magnanimity is the expansion of the soul to great things.
Magnanimous people put themselves in all kinds of danger
for great things, for instance, the common welfare,
justice, divine worship, and so forth.

— Thomas Aquinas

EXPANDING THE SOUL — isn't that a great reason for living and for making the decisions we make? Magnanimity comes from two Latin words: *magna*, which means "great," and *anima*, which means "soul." Thus magnanimity is about having a large soul — not a soul that is puny, the root of *pusillanimity*. With a magnanimous soul we are ready to take on the battles of life; we are spiritual warriors. Included in that warriorship is going to battle on behalf of social justice, the common welfare, and divine worship. How interesting that Aquinas places improving worship on a par with working for the common good and justice. This should give great affirmation to all those attempting to render ritual in forms that work for postmodern people.

Through compassion human beings imitate God.... We find these two things, compassion and justice, in all the works of God.

— Thomas Aquinas

COMPASSION IS OUR VERY IMITATION OF GOD. It is God-like action and God-like being. Aquinas takes seriously the teaching of Jesus that we are to "be compassionate like God in heaven is compassionate" (Luke 6:36). This follows an ancient Jewish teaching that compassion is the secret name for God. There is no better way to demonstrate how God passes through us than carrying out our works of compassion.

Further, compassion and justice are everywhere in the universe, says Aquinas. Justice is about balance, about equilibrium, about homeostasis. We find it in our bodies, in ecosystems, in the movement of planets and stars and the interaction of galaxies. Compassion is the living out of our shared interdependence and interconnectivity. These habits and virtues are everywhere present, "in all the works of God." Are we following in these paths of justice making and compassion?

*All paths lead to God. For God is on them all evenly
for the person who knows with transformed knowledge.*

— Meister Eckhart

HUMANS OFTEN ARGUE, even go to war, over whose path to God is correct. But Eckhart says: Slow down. Breathe. Don't judge. You take your path, and let others take their path. They will all lead to God. What, though, carries us beyond tribalism, beyond egocentricity, which creates those competitive, destructive "My God is better than your God" conflicts? Eckhart says "transformed knowledge." Transformed knowledge comes with meditation, with learning to let go and let be. We must do some inner work to rid ourselves of outer teachings that preach division and exclusion and competition.

I pray God to rid me of God.

— Meister Eckhart

ECKHART OFTEN SURPRISES US with his stark observations. We often make God over into our image, and this is the "God" Eckhart wants removed. Eckhart often prays to God for forgiveness and help moving beyond human projections of God to the real thing. Have you ever prayed God to rid you of God? Are there human projections you need to let go of: perhaps of an all-male God, a God of judgment and condemnation? A God that spreads division, class oppression, homophobia, sexism, excessive nationalism?

God's exit is her entrance.

— Meister Eckhart

THIS IS ANOTHER WAY OF SAYING that when things close down or end in our lives, a new path invariably opens up. The death of a loved one, the death of a relationship, the death of a dream: these are endings, but the hollow spaces left behind are openings, too. Have you ever noticed how new relationships and new possibilities often follow other endings? When in your life have you learned this hard lesson, that "God's exit is her entrance"? Can you trust that when God in one form leaves, God in another form shows up?

One should love God mindlessly.
By this I mean that your soul ought to be without mind
or mental activities or images or representations. Bare your soul
of all mind and stay there without mind.

— Meister Eckhart

HERE ECKHART SPEAKS OF MEDITATION in very Zen-like language. Yet, as with Aquinas before him, there is no evidence that Eckhart was exposed to Buddhism in any way. Thus, the understandings the East has long been known for, the West discovered as well. That is, emptying the mind is a good and wholesome practice. "Bare your soul of all mind and stay there without mind." Your soul is bigger than your mind. It is far more than what we think about: it is our thoughts, and it is all we do not think about. It is nothingness, and it is vastness. So why stay only with your thoughts? Why not entertain your nonthoughts as well? Your nonthoughts can carry you to amazing places. Learn to "love God mindlessly" — sometimes using your mind and sometimes by putting aside your mind.

> *God is not found in the soul by adding anything*
> *but by a process of subtraction.*
>
> — Meister Eckhart

LETTING GO leads us to God experience. Finding God is not about piling spiritual experiences on top of spiritual experiences, but about letting go, subtracting, taking away. Breathe in and breathe out. The breathing out is letting go. As Eckhart says elsewhere, "God is at home. It is we who have gone out for a walk." When have experiences of subtraction in your life revealed to you a deeper presence of God?

Love God as God is — a not-God, a not-mind, a not-person,
a not-image. Love God as God is a pure,
clear One who is separate from all twoness.

— Meister Eckhart

THROUGH RHETORICAL NEGATION, Eckhart describes Aquinas's "Source who has no Source." God is beyond all definitions of God or mind or person or image. God is a "pure, clear One who is separate from all twoness." God is all-encompassing, yet the ultimate in intimacy. Love is that way. A oneing, a union, a communion into which twoness cannot enter. Neither subject nor object. No other. No separateness. No distance. All-present. Have you experienced this kind of union? This is the essence of the mystical experience — the experience of union, of nonduality.

God is a being beyond being and a nothingness beyond being. The most beautiful thing which a person can say about God would be for that person to remain silent from the wisdom of an inner wealth. So, be silent and quit flapping your gums about God.

— Meister Eckhart

WE WANT TO PRAISE GOD, but Eckhart says to "quit flapping your gums." Ouch. Yet Eckhart is calling attention to the limits of language and our human understanding. In the presence of the silence of God, the "nothingness" of God, the transcendence of God, what is there for us to say? To experience the Godhead is to be bathed in mystery (as distinct from history and creation, liberation or redemption, which are the work of God). The Godhead deserves our attention, and we approach and honor it through silence more than through words.

Have you experienced such deep silences in your life? Did you seek these moments, or did they find you? Did they transform, heal, empower, or surprise you? Why is silence so special? "I will call you out the wilderness and there speak to you heart to heart" says God to the prophet Hosea. Can you foster the relationship of silence and heart talk in your life?

Now I shall say something I have never said before. God enjoys himself/ herself. In the same enjoyment in which God enjoys the Godself, God enjoys all creatures. With the same enjoyment with which God enjoys the Godself, God enjoys all creatures, not as creatures, but as God. In the same enjoyment in which God enjoys the Godself, God enjoys all things.

— Meister Eckhart

ECKHART RECOGNIZES AND CELEBRATES the joy God takes in creatures, indeed in all things. Just as we are often asked to see all creatures as a mirror of God, God also sees the Godself in all creatures — and this is the source of the divine delight. Is this not the artist celebrating both the making and what's made? Do these observations give you permission to find God in all things and to take joy and pleasure in these things?

God and his Godhead are as different as heaven and earth. I will go still further: The inner and the outer person are as different as heaven and earth. But God's distance from the Godhead is many thousand miles greater still. God becomes and ceases to become, God waxes and wanes....God and the Godhead are distinguished through deeds and a lack of deeds.

— Meister Eckhart

ECKHART DISTINGUISHES BETWEEN "God" and "Godhead." God names the active side of Divinity — creation, liberation, action, history. Godhead names the being side of Divinity — silence, mystery, darkness, source. In Eckhart's languages (Latin and German), *God* is masculine and *Godhead* is feminine. He decries the exclusive language of God that ignores the Godhead, or that which puts action above being and celebrates history but not mystery. He alerts us to become aware of sexist language when speaking of Divinity. Patriarchy leaves out the Godhead; it leaves out (or utterly distorts) mysticism. Mysticism takes us into the Godhead, whence we come and to which we will return.

God neither heeds nor needs vigils, fasting, prayer, and all forms of mortification in contrast to repose. God needs nothing more than for us to offer him a quiet heart. Then he accomplishes in the soul such secrets and divine deeds that no creature can serve them or even add to them.... The divine nature is repose and God seeks to draw all creatures with him back again to their origin which is repose.

— Meister Eckhart

ECKHART TELLS US that spiritual practice is less about deeds than about repose, which is resting in being itself. Being with being. It is about emptying ourselves, being unmoved, being at peace. Employing a "quiet heart" can take us deeper into the divine nature than elaborate rituals and practices. Repose is our origin. It calls us. We can and ought to return there regularly.

For a human being to possess true poverty, he or she must be as free of his or her created will as they were when they did not yet exist.... People should be as free of their own knowledge as when they were not yet, letting God accomplish whatever God wills. People should stand empty....Following the way of my unborn being I have always been, I am now, and shall remain eternally. What I am by my [temporal] birth is destined to die and be annihilated, for it is mortal; therefore it must with time pass away. In my [eternal] birth all things were born, and I was cause of myself and of all things.

— Meister Eckhart

HAVE YOU BEEN TO THESE AMAZING PLACES that Eckhart speaks of — reconnecting to your "unborn being"? Eckhart believes we all can — and should — visit that place on a regular basis, for it is where we become young again and refreshed and strong. Healthy meditation and real emptying take us there. And when we arrive there we drink in our true freedom, the kind of freedom we entertained before we were born. We begin to taste eternity.

The just person lives in God and God in him. Thus God will be born in this just person and the just person is born into God; and therefore God will be born through every virtue of the just person and will rejoice through every virtue of the just person. And not only at every virtue will God rejoice, but especially at every work of the just person, however small it is. When this work is done through justice and results in justice, God will rejoice at it, indeed, God will rejoice through and through; for nothing remains in God's ground which does not tickle God through and through out of joy.

— Meister Eckhart

CAN WE IMAGINE even the smallest act of compassion, of justice, tickling God to joyous laughter? Is that not reward enough? In this light, what have you done lately to tickle God through and through and move God to rejoice? How busy are you making justice and compassion happen?

> *What happens to another,*
> *whether it be a joy or a sorrow,*
> *happens to me.*
>
> — Meister Eckhart

THIS MAY BE THE MOST SUCCINCT DEFINITION of compassion that I know. Compassion is about our interconnectivity; it's acting out of connection, not competition or ego projection. Thus, your joy is my joy; your sorrow is my sorrow. The former gets us to celebrate together. The latter to struggle to heal, to remove the pain, to share solidarity, or to make justice happen. Whether experiencing joy or sorrow, the heart of compassion is recognizing unity. We share the deepest things — joy and grief, via positiva and via negativa.

All gifts of nature and of grace have been given us on loan. Their ownership is not ours, but God's.... Treat all things as if they were loaned to you without any ownership — whether body or soul, sense or strength, external goods or honors, friends or relations, house or hall, everything. For if I want to possess the property I have instead of receive it on loan, then I want to be a master.

— Meister Eckhart

ECKHART IS SPEAKING OF LETTING GO, or detachment. If we saw our whole lives in the context of their finiteness (death), we would realize we are only here a short while, so to put all our energy into things that pass is foolish. Therefore a consciousness not of ownership but of borrowing makes more sense. It teaches us to respect the earth, as it is not ours to exploit, but it is only ours to maintain, on loan from future generations.

You ask me what the human soul is? No human science can ever fathom what the soul is in its depth. What the soul is in its ground, no one knows. But this we do know: The soul is where God works compassion.

— Meister Eckhart

OUR SOULS ARE DEEPLY MYSTERIOUS and deeply unknowable. Today we would say they contain the unconscious. But the key to it, in Eckhart's eyes, is that it is the place where compassion happens. We might also turn this around and say: we do not truly have soul until we are instruments of divine compassion. Is this a challenge to our species? Is this why so many spiritual teachers, from Buddha to Isaiah, from Muhammad to Lao Tsu, from Jesus to the Dalai Lama, call us to compassion? Compassion is the fullness of being human. It is proof we have a soul.

We are fellow helpers with God, co-creators in everything we do. When Word and work are returned to their source and origin, then all work is accomplished divinely in God. And there too the soul loses itself in a wonderful enchantment.

— Meister Eckhart

ECKHART HONORS OUR WORK PROFOUNDLY. So long as it derives from the Source, we are "co-creators" with God "in everything we do." Divinity is integral to our work. And in addition, a kind of "wonderful enchantment" ensues. Does this correspond to your experience of work? Does this idea lend a new sense of respect for all the work you do — from feeding the kids to cleaning the house to making a living to exercising your citizenship?

The outward work will never be puny if the inward work is great. And the outward work can never be great or even good if the inward one is puny or of little worth. The inward work invariably includes in itself all expansiveness, all breadth, all length, all depth. Such a work receives and draws all its being from nowhere else except from and in the heart of God.

— Meister Eckhart

THERE IS INNER WORK and there is outer work. They relate to each other. But the inner work comes first — our intentions, our motivations, our deepest goals, the via positiva and the via negativa. The deeper we travel, the healthier our outer work. The inner work takes us beyond the work world to the cosmos itself. That is how large our souls are. All authentic work so inspired derives from and in "the heart of God." At work today, can you try to experience this connection?

All works are surely dead if anything from the outside compels you to work.... If your works are to live, then God must move you from the inside, from the innermost region of the soul — then they will really live. There is your life and there alone you live and our works live.

— Meister Eckhart

IF OUR WORK IS COMPELLED only from the outside, that is not enough; this would be, in Eckhart's terms, the very definition of a dead-end job. To feel alive in our work, and for our work to live, we must operate "from the innermost region of the soul." Real work comes from being moved from the inside. This helps us see how valuable it is to explore those innermost regions. It distinguishes a job (getting a paycheck) from work (the reason we are here, giving our gift to the community).

God will be born in the just person just as the just person is born into God. For the just person, to act justly is to live; justice is her life; her being alive, her being to the very extent that she is just.... Compassion means justice.... Compassion is where peace and justice kiss.

— Meister Eckhart

JUSTICE IS SO PROFOUND that it takes over our being, our life, our being alive. In our lifetimes, many people, especially in South and Central America, have given their lives for justice's sake. In addition, we give birth to God or the Christ by our works of healing and justice and compassion.

Some people equate compassion with pity, but this is not the biblical tradition nor is it Eckhart's understanding. Compassion is not to be sentimentalized — it has teeth to it; "compassion means justice." Indeed, compassion is the coming together of peace and justice, which Eckhart beautifully signifies as a mutual kiss of the two. Do you experience this kiss on a regular basis? Do you encourage it in others?

Spirituality is not to be learned by flight from the world, by running away from things, or by turning solitary and going apart from the world. Rather, we must learn an inner solitude wherever or with whomsoever we may be. We must learn to penetrate things and find God there.

— Meister Eckhart

ECKHART ENCOURAGES US TO LEARN "an inner solitude" and to carry that wherever we go. Then we are always in the right place at the right time. He says we don't need a retreat from the world to find this solitude; rather, we must find it within the chaos and confusion and stress that often define the world. Can you access and carry with you this lifesaver of inner solitude wherever you go?

What good is it to me if Mary gave birth to the Son of God 1400 years ago and I do not give birth to the Son of God in my own person and time and culture? ... We are all meant to be mothers of God.

— Meister Eckhart

WITH TYPICAL BLUNTNESS, Eckhart seems to be asking us to reconsider Christmas. For Eckhart, Christmas is not just about celebrating the birth of Jesus as the son of God; it loses meaning if it doesn't also celebrate our ongoing birth as sons and daughters of God. Moreover, Mary is not unique. We are all meant to be "other Marys," or mothers of God. We all birth the Christ in our work and in our being and personhood. This teaching makes for a very unsentimental Christmas but one filled with responsibility.

Readers today think exclusively of Jesus when they hear the words the "Son of God." But the phrase had a life of its own before it was applied to Jesus...referring to angels (Genesis 6:2), the whole people called Israel (Hosea 11:1), and the king in David's line (Psalm 2:7). Direct revelation extends God's favor to people and angels; each is "the Son," "the beloved," as Jesus became in his vision at his baptism (Mark 1:11).

Baptism, in fact, was when, according to Paul, God sends the Spirit of his Son into every believer, who cries to God, "Abba, Father" (Galatians 4:6). The believer becomes a Son, just as Jesus called upon his father; as Paul says in the same sentence, God sends his Spirit "because you are Sons." The moment of baptism, the supreme moment of faith, was when one discovered oneself as a Son of God, because Jesus as God's Son was disclosed in one's heart.

— Bruce Chilton

I ONCE MET A RABBI who said to me, "In my tradition, anyone who truly lives a life of wisdom can be called a 'Son of God.' For that reason I have no problem calling Jesus a Son of God." When Christians, often in the name of proselytizing or building up empires, emphasize too much the divinity of Jesus, much is lost. We are all God's sons and daughters, and this was the teaching of Jesus and even of Paul. But often we have missed that basic message in the Christian faith. Mystics call us back to this truth.

In all faces is seen the Face of faces, veiled in a billion riddles — yet unveiled it is not seen, until, at last, above all faces we enter into a certain secret and mystical silence where there is no knowledge of a face.

— Nicolas of Cusa

THE FIFTEENTH-CENTURY MYSTIC and scientist Nicolas of Cusa speaks in paradoxical language of the riddle of the mirror: how our small *f* faces reflect the big *F* Face of God. Yet even when unveiled, God's Face remains unseen. Every face mirrors something of Divinity, and yet we cannot describe what Divinity looks like. God is seen but not seen. Creatures who are faces of God reveal God but they do not reveal God. Then, when we do enter into the silent and mysterious divine presence, we enter a place beyond faces and individuality. Nothingness remains. And that takes us still closer to the Divine Face.

This mist, this cloud, this darkness into which we go, transcending knowledge, is the path below which your face cannot be found except veiled; but it is that very darkness which reveals your face is there, beyond all veils.

— Nicolas of Cusa

CUSA ANTICIPATES PSYCHOANALYTIC EXPLORATION into the unconscious when he speaks of journeying to a place of darkness and transcending knowledge and the veiling of our face. But the darkness is welcoming; it holds a revelation, an unveiling of our true selves, of our authentic face. This is another way of talking of the dark night of the soul, which has so much truth to teach us. Have you made this journey yourself? Would you dare to journey to find the unveiled face within your darker self?

O God, the longer I gaze upon your face, the more acutely do you seem to turn the gaze of your eyes upon me!... Thus, when I meditate on how that face is truth and the best measure of all faces, I am expanded into a state of immense wonder....

Those who look upon you with a loving face will find your face looking on them with love.... Those who look upon you in hate will similarly find your face hateful. Those who gaze at you in joy will find your face joyfully reflected back at them.

— Nicolas of Cusa

CUSA ECHOES ECKHART'S OBSERVATION that "the eye with which I see God is the same eye with which God sees me." The face-to-face gaze we experience with God certainly inspires wonder — a pure subject-to-subject gaze, with no objects — but Eckhart teaches that "all the names we give to God come from an understanding of ourselves." Thus, the quality of the gaze depends on what we bring to the encounter, on the quality of our being.

In speaking of love or hate emanating from God's face, is Cusa teaching about karma? Put out love and you receive love; put out hate and you conjure up hate; put out joy and joy is reflected back to you. Does this match your experience?

O Divine One, all beauty which can be conceived is less than the beauty of your face.

   Though every face is beautiful, no face is beauty's self but your face, God/dess, has beauty and this having is being.

   It is absolute beauty itself, which is the form that gives being to every beautiful form.

— Nicolas of Cusa

CUSA REVEALS HIS UNDERSTANDING of the importance of beauty in our understanding of Divinity. Only God's face is beauty itself, but this is the beauty not of appearance or form but of being. God does not have beauty as creatures do. God's being, "absolute beauty itself," is the source for "every beautiful form." Thus beauty is a worthy path to God. And God wants it that way. Can you recognize in all forms the beautiful expression of God's being?

*Anyone who understands that the great variety of things
is a reflected image of the one God and leaves behind the diversity
in all the images will arrive in an incomprehensible manner
at the incomprehensible.*

— Nicolas of Cusa

LEAVE BEHIND "the diversity in all the images," counsels Cusa; it's hard to comprehend how to do this, and yet this very simple path is the only one leading to the incomprehensible. This is a basic teaching about meditation. Let the particulars go; let self go. Sink into nothingness, the void, silence, darkness, where no image shines. In the darkness deep encounters happen. The incomprehensible speaks its own language amid the silence of things.

Divinity is the enfolding of the universe,
and the universe is the unfolding of divinity....

The human mind
is the enfolding of its own dream world
and its own dream world is the unfolding of the human mind.

Divinity
is the enfolding and unfolding of
everything that is.
Divinity is in all things in such a way
that all things are in divinity.

Mind itself
supposing itself to encompass, survey,
and comprehend all things
thus concludes
that it is in everything
and everything is in it.

— Nicolas of Cusa

CUSA LIKES VERY MUCH TO PLAY with the themes of enfolding and unfolding. There is a Möbius strip–like infinite-loop quality to this dynamic — expanding and contracting, embracing and revealing — that plays out on every level. The human mind both enfolds its dream world and unfolds as it does so. In creation at large, God is the enfolding of the universe and the universe is the unfolding of Divinity. And God is also the enfolding of all things while, in panentheistic fashion, all things are in God. Have you experienced this sense of endless connection, flowing in and out?

When indeed the human mind, the clear likeness of God, partici-
pates as it is able in the fertility of the creative nature, it puts forth
from itself, as the image of the divine form, symbolic entities in the
likeness of real beings.

Thus, the human mind is the form of the symbolic world, just as
the Divine Mind is that of the real world.

— Nicolas of Cusa

LIKE AQUINAS, CUSA IS COMPARING human creativity to that
of the Spirit of God, or the Divine Mind at work in the world.
Humans participate in "the fertility of the creative nature" of
God. That is what it means to be made in the image and likeness of God. It means we are in touch with our creativity, and
we respect and honor it in others.

Like Aquinas, Cusa attributes human creativity to our likeness to the Divine Artist. We reflect the divine creativity and
art. We see once again how important creativity was to the premodern consciousness. Modern consciousness has not given it
this profound setting. We thus reduce and manipulate creativity
strictly for commercial success — to sell goodies, to make ce-
lebrities, and to build the human ego.

Peace is the bearing of fruit of the mind. It is the dwelling place of divinity, the divine locus.... Contemplation is living in peace.

— Nicolas of Cusa

CONTEMPLATION BRINGS PEACE. It is "living in peace." Peace is the fruition of the work of the mind. We seek peace. Eckhart says we "run into peace." All things seek peace or repose. Divinity dwells there. We taste that peace in contemplation. We taste the divine presence.

The Logos of creation in whom all things were created can be nothing other than divine wisdom. Thus it is that wisdom is eternal, for it precedes every beginning and all created reality.

— Nicolas of Cusa

CUSA CONNECTS THE COSMIC CHRIST as Logos (or Word) with the Cosmic Christ as wisdom. They are the same. Wisdom precedes all beginnings and all creation. Wisdom was there from before the beginning of the world.

Humanity will find that it is not a diversity of creeds, but the very same creed which is everywhere proposed.

There cannot but be one wisdom. If it were possible to have many wisdoms these would have to be from one; for before any plurality exists there must first be unity.

Humans must therefore all agree that there is but one most simple wisdom whose power is infinite; and everyone, in explaining the intensity of this beauty, must discover that it is a supreme and terrible beauty.

— Nicolas of Cusa

I SEE CUSA SPEAKING from the fifteenth century to the movement of deep ecumenism in our time. He says that while humans profess various creeds, there is really only one creed, and that is wisdom. Wisdom is simple yet infinite, and to apprehend it is to recognize a "supreme and terrible beauty." This beauty is not the same as "pretty"; it relates to awe and even terror.

Cusa challenges us to move beyond parochial creeds to recognize this one supreme and terrible beauty that is wisdom. Are we up to his challenge?

The Lord of Sky and Earth has heard the groans of those who have been slaughtered and imprisoned and reduced to slavery and who suffer because of religious wars.... The Creator is moved with compassion towards humanity and will try to guide all the variety of religions to one greater unimpeachable harmony in which all opinion is one.

— Nicolas of Cusa

CUSA IS DECRYING the price innocent people have so often paid for violent religious crusades and pogroms and inquisitions. He promises that God will eventually clean up religion and move it beyond warfare and conquest and proselytizing to a "greater unimpeachable harmony." In the meantime, how are we doing?

Wisdom
is shouting in the streets.
It is simply not enough
for those seeking wisdom
merely to read about it.
Wisdom must be discovered.

And once discovered
it must be learned by heart.
You will not find wisdom in your books
for it is not of your books,
but of the books of our God/dess.

What are these books?
They are those which the Divine has written
with her own finger.

Where can they be found?

Everywhere!

— Nicolas of Cusa

LIKE PREMODERN THINKERS EVERYWHERE, Cusa does not consider literal books and human words adequate for understanding God's Word. As it is to Aquinas and Eckhart and Francis of Assisi, to Cusa the book of nature is just as important as human books. You don't read about wisdom so much as you search it out in the streets; you discover it everywhere and in everything. It is available to all. Literacy is no test of spirituality.

> *Because in all speech divinity is unexpressible,*
> *there can be no limit to the means of expressing it.*
>
> — Nicolas of Cusa

FIRST, CUSA ACKNOWLEDGES what Aquinas and Eckhart do: that God has no proper name. No word can properly identify God. "In all speech divinity is unexpressible." On the other hand, this means everything is a name for God. Everything and no thing. All beings express Divinity and all efforts can express Divinity. Yet all fall short as well.

The scholars are deficient in that they are afraid to enter the darkness. Reason shuns it and is afraid to steal in. But in avoiding the darkness reason does not arrive at a vision of the invisible....Divinity is the coincidence of opposites.

— Nicolas of Cusa

TWO CENTURIES before the period we call the "Enlightenment,[Cusa warns us of the dangers of a cult of rationality, and he criticizes scholars as afraid of the dark, afraid of places that reason cannot enter.] In this way, he invites us to enter the dark, to seek the incomprehensible, to look for the invisible there (this is the "apophatic" Divinity). Balancing the God of light with the God of darkness is an expression of "the coincidence of opposites." This is one more reason why reason alone has trouble apprehending Divinity. Paradox often names Divinity best.

Divinity is the alpha and the omega, the beginning and the end, the macrocosm and the microcosm, the yin and the yang, the dark and the light, the soft and the hard — the coming together of the dynamic of opposites. This takes us beyond left-brain thinking to more inclusive, right-brain thinking.

The relationship of our intellect to the truth is like that of a polygon to a circle: the resemblance to the circle grows with the multiplication of the angles of the polygon; but short of the polygon actually becoming a circle, no multiplication of its angles, even if it were infinite, will make the polygon equal the circle.

It is therefore clear that all we know of truth is that the Absolute Truth, as it is, is beyond our grasp.

The more mindfully we learn this lesson of ignorance, the closer we draw to truth itself.

— Nicolas of Cusa

WE APPROACH TRUTH but we do not seize absolute truth, which is "beyond our grasp." This ought to make us a bit humble and our ways humble; it ought to inspire humility. We need to carry this "lesson of ignorance" with us at all times, for this awareness will itself draw us closer to truth.

Clearly, Cusa sees no human thought or system as upholding all truth. He is a champion of limits. Do you agree with his analogy? What happens when groups or individuals ignore this teaching and see their understanding as the only absolute truth? What dangers unfold from that?

It is necessary for one who wants to attain understanding to raise the intellect above the meaning of words rather than to insist upon their properties which, in any case, cannot be properly adapted to such great mindful mysteries.

Intellectual knowledge, alone and unaided,
desires and exaggerates
*   the victory of words*
and it is far from that
to God
who is our peace.

— Nicolas of Cusa

THE INTELLECT by itself "exaggerates the victory of words." Have you ever found this to be true? Have you ever had moments when language and logic failed — whether to resolve a dilemma or to reach an understanding? Do you always pray with words, or do you sometimes reach out wordlessly? Has a painting ever communicated to you without words? As Cusa observes, it's worth training our intellect to rise "above the meaning of words" in its effort to touch the "great mindful mysteries," for the God of peace is far from the place of words.

The universe is in each person in such a way that each person is in it. And so every person in the universe is the universe.

— Nicolas of Cusa

WE THE MICROCOSM carry the macrocosm in us quite literally. Cusa is offering us not only a mystical insight but also an accurate description of today's science. We now know that the whole universe and everything in it began with a cell smaller than a zygote, and this cell became the fireball, and the fireball birthed hydrogen and helium atoms, which became galaxies and supernovas and stars and planets...and our home, mother earth. Quite literally, we are in the universe and the universe is in us.

Every creature, as such, is perfect even if by comparison with others it may seem imperfect. None desires greater nobility than any other; each loves that nobility which God has given it while striving to maintain and intensify that nobility....Every creature is, so to speak, a "God-creature," a "Finite-infinity." Which means that no creature's existence could be more perfect than it is.

— Nicolas of Cusa

THERE IS A NOBILITY TO EVERY SPECIES, which derives from each species' own self-defined perfection. In that context, life is not a survival-of-the-fittest competition among beings, nor do humans possess "greater nobility." All creatures are only busy being the best that they can be, "while striving to maintain and intensify that nobility." That is the push in evolution, which applies equally to all, not one over others. Evolution is the quest for perfection or for bringing out the best in ourselves, the nobility of ourselves.

Wonder is the reason we seek to know any reality whatsoever.

— Nicolas of Cusa

CUSA IS VERY MUCH ON THE SIDE OF AQUINAS, and he reflects the premodern consciousness that considers wonder the starting place of philosophy. It is wonder that drives us to know, not doubt, as Descartes and modern consciousness postulated. Wonder leads to wisdom and to satisfaction and delight. Learning is a joy! Yet is our educational system teaching these things? Do we have a wonder-based curriculum? Do you approach learning with joy? Are young people learning these things in school?

I experience your wisdom, my God,
which not only does not condemn me as a miserable sinner,
but sweetly feeds me with distinct desire.

— Nicolas of Cusa

LIKE JULIAN, Cusa invokes desire as that which most sweetly feeds us. Not condemnation, nor an image of ourselves as sinners, but the journey of desire takes us to what is beautiful and full of grace. Where are your desires taking you these days? Are you in touch with your deepest desires?

My Beloved is the mountains,
And lonely wooded valleys,
Strange islands,
And resounding rivers,
The whistling of love-stirring breezes,

The tranquil night
At the time of the rising dawn,
Silent music,
Sounding solitude,
The supper that refreshes, and deepens love.

— John of the Cross

THIS PASSAGE IS FROM JOHN OF THE CROSS'S great poem "Canticle." Throughout the poem the poet searches for his lost beloved. John began writing the poem while he was imprisoned by his Carmelite brothers for daring to call for a reformation in his order (as Teresa had done in her Carmelite order for women). The lover searches everywhere, over hills and through valleys, forests, and cities, and finally he finds his beloved: "My Beloved is the mountains."

"Beloved" is John's favorite name for God (as it was for Rumi, the great Sufi mystic). Yet his beloved is not hiding in the mountains and the valleys and the islands and the rivers — his beloved *is* the mountains, valleys, islands, and rivers. This is raw panentheism.

God is also paradoxical — the Beloved is "silent music" and "sounding solitude." And God is a refreshing supper that "deepens love."

Have you ever lost God, only to find God again in nature? What paradox captures or names your own divine experiences?

Although I have spoken here only of seven Mansions yet in each there are comprised many more, both above and below and around, with lovely gardens and fountains and things so delectable that you will want to lose yourselves in praise of the great God Who created it in His image and likeness.

— Teresa of Avila

IN HER BOOK *The Interior Castle*, Teresa of Avila leads us on a journey to explore the seven "mansions," or rooms, that make up our souls. This quote comes at the end of her book, where she points out how rich and diverse our souls are. Even after all she has described, there is much more to explore — "above and below and around," amazing endless spaces within our souls that will render us lost in praise. Have you made this journey, wandering among the mansions and gardens of your soul? What does your soul's architecture, made in God's image and likeness, look like? If you haven't visited yet, what is holding you back?

The modern economy is propelled by a frenzy of greed and indulges in an orgy of envy, and these are not accidental features but the very causes of its expansionist success....If human vices such as greed and envy are systematically cultivated, the inevitable result is nothing less than a collapse of intelligence.

— E. F. Schumacher

E. F. SCHUMACHER, well known for his work *Small Is Beautiful*, was a British economist and head of planning for the British Coal Board during the mid-twentieth century. He also studied Gandhi, nonviolence, ecology, and Buddhism along with Christianity. He is speaking ancient wisdom when he points out that the "capital sins" of greed and envy are simply not sustainable. When he talks of these being "cultivated," he is referring to our media and advertising-saturated age. Do you agree with him that advertising mania results in a "collapse of intelligence"?

Similarly, Rabbi Abraham Heschel once said that if we "forfeit our sense of awe, the universe becomes a market place." Are divine awe and the marketplace incompatible? Does the cultivation of greed kill mysticism?

Strange to say, the Sermon on the Mount gives pretty precise instructions on how to construct an outlook that could lead to an Economics of Survival.

— How blessed are those who know that they are poor: the kingdom of Heaven is theirs.

— How blessed are the sorrowful;
They shall find consolation.

— How blessed are those of a gentle spirit;
They shall have the earth for their possession.

— How blessed are those who hunger and thirst to see right prevail;
They shall be satisfied;

— How blessed are the peacemakers;
God shall call them his sons.

It may seem daring to connect these beatitudes with matters of technology and economics but may it not be that we are in trouble precisely because we have failed for so long to make this connection?
It is not difficult to discern what these beatitudes may mean for us today:

— We are poor, not demigods.

— We have plenty to be sorrowful about, and are not emerging into a golden age.

— We need a gentle approach, a non-violent spirit, and small is beautiful.

— We must concern ourselves with justice and see right prevail.

And all this, only this, can enable us to become peacemakers.

— E. F. Schumacher

Do you agree with Schumacher that the Beatitudes make a solid foundation for an economics of survival and for a sustainable economics? Why or why not? How do we go about implementing such a philosophy of economics?

Can you agree with each of these observations by Schumacher? Is he correct that this is the only path to peacemaking?

Education is the most vital of all resources. If Western civilization is in a state of permanent crisis, it is not far fetched to suggest that there may be something wrong with its education.

"Know-how" is no more a culture than a piano is music. Can education helps us to ... turn the potentiality into a reality to the benefit of man?

To do so, the task of education would be, first and foremost, the transmission of ideas of value, of what to do with our lives.... More education can help us only if it produces more wisdom.

The essence of education, I suggested, is the transmission of values.... They are the very instruments through which we look at, interpret, and experience the world.

— E. F. Schumacher

IT'S BEEN NEARLY FORTY YEARS since Schumacher described Western civilization as being in a "state of permanent crisis." Has anything changed in that time? If "education is the most vital of all resources," how are we doing? If transmitting values lies at the heart of education, how do we bring a values-based education to the fore?

Poetry has meant a great deal in my life. That sensitivity, that intuition, an attitude of tenderness before nature, before all things, before people, before pain, before weakness, before pettiness, at times and under circumstances of exaltation also. I therefore believe that poetry has been for me much more than a hobby. It has been a psychological constituent, which has expressed me and through which I have expressed my faith and even my ministry.

— Bishop Pedro Casaldaliga

BISHOP PEDRO SPEAKS OF THE SENSITIVITY and tenderness that poetry brings to his work and faith. Is poetry important to you? What poets feed your soul, your prayer, your spirit? If not through poetry, how do you bring your sensitivity, intuition, tenderness toward nature into play in your inner life?

Every poet is a prophet....Every poet listens to the heart of the people and translates it into a cry, an outcry. All poets give to their people...the word, the vision, the climate that makes the people vibrate, that gives it life. And the Bible itself has shown us that all prophets are poets. Moreover, I believe that depending on the sensitivity that one has, grace moves within one and acts within one. It is evident that in what is mathematical, grace will express itself mathematically, in experiences, in projects, in performances more certain, more exact, more precise. And in the person who is a poet, grace expresses itself in a poetic way.

— Bishop Pedro Casaldaliga

BISHOP PEDRO SAYS that every poet is a prophet, and vice versa, both crystalizing a vision of life and grace that moves people. However, Rabbi Heschel teaches that a prophet is "one who interferes." Are these in fact the same? What prophet/poets awaken you and show you how grace often interferes in the everyday way of the world? Who translates your heart into an outcry, perhaps steering you in new directions? How does the poet in you express itself?

I am thinking more and more that God will not judge us either for the good or the evil that we have done, but simply for whether we have been capable of accepting God's love and transmitting it to other people.... Yes, I must begin by giving thanks to God for everything, because really everything has been the grace of God. And above all for what final great grace that has been now ten years in a row of suffering, of struggles, of persecutions, of anguish, of throbbing, of enthusiasms, of people, of church, of faith, of hope in this beloved Mato Grosso, this Amazonia, this church of Brazil, of Latin America.

— Bishop Pedro Casaldaliga

MANY HAVE BEEN THE SUFFERINGS of the people of Latin America. Numerous martyrs have shed their blood and died there for the cause of justice. One person I met in Bishop Pedro's diocese told me he knew "at least ten off the top of my head." I myself have known a few personally. Bishop Pedro has been a witness to much of that history. We should be grateful and proud of the courage these people have manifested, just as we are for the earliest Christians who paid the ultimate price for standing up to the Roman Empire.

Despite this history, Bishop Pedro says our task in life is relatively simple: Accept God's love and transmit it to other people. How are we doing? What are the obstacles that hold us back?

I became Christian because it carries the full potentiality of the indigenous; it gives me the overview, the center of vision, to make the recovery. You can look at it historically, to see if Christianity was developed enough in the medieval period, to match the indigenous. You could take the lines of the mystics and the saints, and correlate them with the holy men. The greatness of Christianity is its capacity to assimilate whatever the findings of the human spirit are. Christ was the central archetype of the union between God and man.

— William Everson

POET WILLIAM EVERSON PRAISES CHRISTIANITY for its capacity to assimilate many strands of the history of spirit. One sociologist has observed that while the holy book of Islam, the Quran, was written and is learned in one language, Arabic, the Christian Bible from the start has been multicultural. Though they described the experiences of Jewish people, the Gospels and Epistles were written in Greek, not Hebrew. So Christianity was launched quite fully into a foreign, or gentile, world from its early beginnings.

Everson sees a profound connection between medieval Christianity and indigenous consciousness. Both share a premodern view of the world. Indeed, both are steeped in a mystical experience of the Divine, which is why so many mystics in this book are medieval Christians.

Do you agree with Everson that Christ represents an archetype of the union between God and man?

I would say that the vision quest offers more direct access to the Animal Powers than Christianity does; for in our civilization we have cut ourselves off from the roots of our instincts. Christianity in the thirteenth century still maintained this primitivism, the source of its vision; it had found its mind, seized the Greek thought, an achievement the aboriginals could never match.

— William Everson

EVERSON BELIEVES that animal powers give us access to our instinctual roots and that modern Christianity, unlike medieval Christianity, has wandered far from our instincts and into our heads almost exclusively. In your life, are you more of a modern or medieval Christian? Would you rather pray sitting in a church pew or dancing outdoors in the forest? Would you rather meditate in a cathedral or in a sweat lodge? To connect with the Divine, do you turn to the Bible or a vision quest? Clearly, Everson is not intimidated by pagan-phobia. He recognizes that ancient traditions accomplished some spiritual tasks very well.

Christ was perhaps the greatest of all shamans. Yes. Forty days in the desert, the resurrection, the carrying of the cross, as a Sun Dance.... The link would seem to be the Animal Powers. Christ would relate to the Animal Powers that preceded our more sophisticated religious impulses. He relates to them through his human side, and that's where the full force of it connects.... For the poet, too, everything depends upon the quality and prolongation of the creative trance, within which he is enabled to engage his demons, his obsession.... Out in the "great solitude," the shaman wrestles with the tribal images his people have impounded within him. And hence in the principled solitude of his self-imposed condition of "cunning silence, and exile," the modern poet goes forth to "forge in the smithy of his soul the uncreated conscience of his race."

— William Everson

EVERSON CALLS JESUS A GREAT SHAMAN. A shaman connects two worlds. A shaman has undergone a profound breakthrough that awakens dormant powers of healing and of vision. And a shaman takes on extreme tasks for the sake of the community, that the people may live. The shaman seeks solitude on a regular basis. In all these ways, Jesus was a shaman. Does that change your view of Jesus, or of shamans? If we are followers of Jesus, are we meant to incarnate shamanhood also?

Violence is part of the dynamic of change, springing from a lack of proportion within the multiplicity of things. It is this violence, this wrath, that is divine.... For the Christian, Christ mounted the Cross, accepted violence into Himself, to place the crucial point precisely where it obtains, the point of convergence between the higher and lower octaves of existence, solving its problem once and for all.... As the age secularizes and grows "secure," the violence increases.

— William Everson

BY VIOLENCE EVERSON MEANS the creative life force that is inborn within the individual. If this force of vitality is lacking, in Everson's view, one cannot be truly alive. In this context, another word for *violence* is *wildness*. Everson is underscoring the role of wildness in Jesus' life and choices. Does wildness play a role in your spirituality? In your understanding of Jesus and of the universe? To what degree do you expect creation to be "pretty" and "tame," devoid of all wildness? Do you sometimes resist or rebel at the wild aspects of creation?

Christ took it to the point of physical violence. He reached down to the depths. When he accepted the cross he became more than a poet, he became a saint. As a Christian I was always close to the heart of violence in my unconscious and it came out in my work. It was from Jeffers that I learned the problem of the relevance of violence in Nature. Violence is the ingredient that makes evolution pertinent. The violence that Christ took on was social.

— William Everson

THERE IS A VIOLENCE and wildness in evolution. There is also a violence and wildness in society and empire building. Everson sees Jesus as having taken on the powers of violence of the Roman Empire. His crucifixion was meant to put violence to rest. Does it do that for you? Have we moved beyond social violence and beyond the violence of empires? Consider the lives of Gandhi and Martin Luther King Jr.: Do they represent the true teaching of Jesus that we are capable of substituting compassion for violence?

The secret of vocation is the calling, the spiritual dimension. The vision quest is a seeking of the discovery of one's vocation. It's an act, an activity. It comes from the collective and reenters the culture. The call comes from a collective need. There's a need for doctors, a need for carpenters, all of the activities of economics and entertainment.

— William Everson

WE OFTEN FOCUS on how our jobs and careers serve ourselves, but in what ways are we serving others? Do you sense a calling, a vocation, in the work you do? Can you name the collective need behind the calling? How does your work fulfill the needs of the common good and the greater community?

Violence is the eruption of passivity into act in the material universe, the jostle of forms and unpredictableness of a chaotic world. The world is unified but there is an edge of violence in it — which is the chaos. The evolution of new forms, the evolution of form from a lower to a higher state, these are all addressed to the problem of violence....[Violence is] the central problem in life. Look at Shakespeare, Milton, Dante, Homer especially — the work is saturated with violence. It's the obsessional part of human life that is unsolvable save through the religious dimension. I was preoccupied with Old Testament violence, the relation of violence to the sacred.

— William Everson

EVERSON RECOGNIZES how omnipresent violence is in the world. The universe, after all, is beautiful (not just pretty), and beauty involves terror and violence. The original fireball, earthquakes, volcanoes — we fool ourselves if we think we live in a nonviolent universe. Everson insists on not living in denial about how violent life is, how violent evolution is, how omnipresent chaos is, and how violent great literature is. Such violence is "unsolvable save through the religious dimension." Violence and wildness point toward the sacred.

The nonviolence movements of Gandhi, King, and Mandela would seem to support the role that healthy religion can play. Compassion turns violence around. Do you agree? What good things come from chaos and from violence? Can humans learn to live nonviolently in a violent universe?

It has been our disseverance from the earth that has destroyed the earth. We have to go on a vision quest to neutralize it. The first thing we have to find out is what we are searching for — for we are moving out of emptiness, our spiritual sloth. We are beginning to focus, to see the problem as it is, now. We are focusing on Nature, but it was the Indians who taught us how to focus on the environment to begin with.... We can avoid forsaking the earth by retaining our connection to the primitive and the primal.

— William Everson

ALL MYSTICS SHOW how God is found in creation itself, in nature, and encourage us to encounter the Divine there. However, in modern times, we see that it is not only our personal relationship to God that suffers when we don't. The health of nature and the earth depend on our awakening out of "spiritual sloth." What actions can we take that connect us "to the primitive and the primal"? What forms of ritual are needed at this time to wake us up to the sacredness of nature and the pain of nature? What might our vision quest look like? What is it we are searching for?

The bridge between the sacred and the profane is the problem of greater consciousness. It's as if the main problem of humanity is the division between those two worlds. So far, based upon mysticism, certain special types have evolved to serve the race in helping to make the bridge. But the goal is for everyone to participate in it, and to enjoy it, and all vocations will eventually lead to that.

— William Everson

DO YOU SENSE THIS DIVISION between the sacred and the profane in your life and your spirituality? Who do you know who bridges that divide? Have you done so yourself? To overcome this dualism, what do you think you and those in your community need to do to expand to a greater consciousness?

In animism the Native Americans met the problem of the split in the psyche, between the sacred and the profane, through the spirits of the animals. They embodied the sacred dimension — the birds, the reptiles, and the mammals. They also used the factor of violence to heighten the tempo between the sacred and the profane.

— William Everson

MANY PREMODERN CULTURES held animistic beliefs, and these ideas have largely been discarded in modern religions as pagan. Yet is there a place for animism in your own spiritual practice and perspective today? Since animism encourages a direct relationship with plants and rocks, rivers and mountains, animals and trees — that is, all of God's creation, in which God remains present, according to the mystics — aren't there ways animism could be included as part of your spiritual practice and integrated into your awareness of Christ consciousness?

In that union
Wholeness, the core of Godhead, dawns.

For God grows in them. In the sacramental oneness
Presence flows and possesses; in the unsearchable
Deeps of that contemplation
Spirit abides; they know the wholeness of spirit.
Its mystical knowledge moves into union,
Makes a rapture within, and they worship.
They gaze in worship on the deep God-presence each wakes in the
other,
And night contains them.

   For over the bed
Spirit hovers, and in their flesh
Spirit exults, and at the tips of their fingers
An angelic rejoicing, and where the phallos
Dips in the woman, in the flow of the woman on the phallos-shaft,
The dark God listens.

       —— William Everson

EVERSON'S POEM "RIVER-ROOT" celebrates human lovemaking as a theophany, not unlike the Song of Songs or the temples of India that honor the mystical dimension to sexuality. A "sacramental oneness" is at stake, Spirit abides, contemplation occurs, worship is elicited, and the God-presence is awakened. "The dark God listens," angels rejoice, and "Spirit hovers and exults" during intercourse. Most lovemaking takes place in the dark, in the world of the apophatic, or dark, Divinity. But the withinness of a woman receiving a man's love is another space where Divinity dwells in the dark. Have you ever felt a spiritual aspect in your experience of sexual love? What is your reaction to this contemporary but ancient mystical teaching about sexuality?

> *For the phallus is holy*
> *And holy is the womb: the holy phallus*
> *In the sacred womb. And they melt.*
> *And flowing they merge the incarnational join*
> *Oned with the Christ. The oneness of each*
> *Ones them with God.*

— William Everson

DO YOU BELIEVE THAT THE PHALLUS AND THE WOMB are "holy"? Do you know anyone who's taught that? Is that something you have learned on your own? Are you still learning it? In our culture, this understanding of sexuality is not easy to find. Yet in theological language, according to Everson, this is the very meaning of "incarnational" and being "oned with the Christ." *Incarnation* means "to be made flesh," and we rediscover the holiness of flesh and the holiness of lovemaking in this poem. The lovers are "oned with the Christ" and oned with God because that is what love and lovemaking do.

> For this is the prototypal
> Act of creation. Where the phallus
> Kisses the womb-nerve listening
> The Father is. And as the phallus flows
> So is uttered the Son. And as Father and Son
> Meld together, merging in love,
> So here Spirit flows. Between taut phallus and tremulous womb,
> The male nerve and the female,
> Spirit moves and is one.

— William Everson

LOVEMAKING, THE POET IS SAYING, is an archetype of creation, and within the sexual act he envisions the holy Trinity at work: Father and phallus, Son and flow, and melding and merging are the flowing of the Spirit. Between male and female, lover and beloved, between yin and yang, phallus and womb, the "Spirit moves and is one." Is this one reason why sexuality is so important in our lives — that it takes us back to our Source, back to the trinitarian acts of creation?

How long they lie each never knows.
This prayer, their one worship. A worship
Learned in the years. For youth leans on them:
They are getters of children: known much and have suffered.
In the deeps of the soul have ached for each other,
Accepting suffering . . .

And now in their night
They know the incarnational join: body to body
Twain in one flesh . . .

Out in the night the River runs.

— William Everson

THESE ARE NOT FIRST-TIME LOVERS. They have lived together, raised a family, suffered the give-and-take, the wins and losses of building a home together. But their lovemaking is their prayer; it is their worship that has been perfected through years together.

Do you believe that lovemaking becomes more profound, more prayerful and worshiplike when you and your lover have traveled through suffering together?

The poet sets his poem "River-Root" in the context of the great Mississippi River running through the night. The river never ceases to run, to give. It is always giving, always on the move, always pouring itself out. Lovemaking takes place in a cosmic context, in the broad setting of nature's other acts of lovemaking. Ours is not an isolated act; it is what nature does, carrying life from generation to generation, carrying love ever onward, ever wet, ever new.

Suddenly the world
Cracks, the phallos
Slams home, slams the ineluctable stroke.
And the universe splits, the touched-off tinder,
Fired by that blaʒing torch
Detonates all the tamped and pounded down empacted intensity.

— William Everson

THERE IS A WILDNESS AND VIOLENCE to love and lovemaking, and there comes a moment of crescendo and climax where "the world cracks" and "the universe splits." Clearly our sexuality is a cosmic event not only because orgasm feels like a great rupture but because, indeed, it is an evolutionary development, a cosmic invention having emerged some one billion years ago. Since then, sexuality has brought about a lot of changes in the universe, number one being the increase of diversity, the shaking up of genes and much more rapid changes in evolution. Later, the poet says that "universal galaxies" sweep through the loins of the male. An "empacted intensity" is part of those changes. Love is a kind of empacted intensity.

And the finger of God
Inscribes on the uterine wall of night
Its prophecy of life ...

In the drenched flesh, in the fabric beyond the flesh,
They have touched transcendence, a syzygy
Greater than wonder ever could know.
There is nothing other.

— William Everson

THE FINGER OF GOD is writing on the walls of the uterus: Life can take hold there. A prophecy of life is spelled out. Transcendence has been tasted and touched in the act of mutual love, giving and receiving. A syzygy of tremendous wonder has taken place.

Is that your experience also? How would you describe the miracle and the mystery of procreation? Has the poet helped to name your experience of the mystical side of lovemaking?

In the essential speechlessness that mysticism is, poetry finds its voice. Like prayer, it moves forever beyond itself to its own extinction. Then it gives up gladly, relinquishing the substance of itself in what it was created to achieve. This is a feature it shares with physical love. In the storm and rapture of the embrace, love transcends itself by centering itself. The phallus knocking at the womb, like the tongue stuttering in the throat, achieves at climax that expenditure which is its failure, the quintessence of success. I think more than any other form of art, poetry is mysticism's flesh.

— William Everson

EVERSON SEES MYSTICISM as "essential speechlessness." Do you agree? He is talking about the via negativa and the letting go of all images and all words; silence lies at the heart of mysticism. Thus, the goal of a poem or a prayer is to move the person beyond words, resulting in the "extinction" of the poem, the prayer. Have you experienced this paradox of words leading to an awe beyond words?

Everson also speaks of lovemaking as taking us beyond words, into realms of transcendence. "Poetry is mysticism's flesh." What do you think of that observation?

In the extremes of imagination the poet and the saint concur....
Poetry, like sanctity, is the orchestration of multiple attributes into
vast, compelling wholes.... The mystic speaks. What impels him is
his whole incentive, the fascination. Obsessed by enchantment, tan-
talized by the imperceptible, he yields up his reason to his instinct,
and his instinct, liberated, guides his intelligence....Fructification
takes him. He grapples God on earth, God in the sea, God in the sky.
He smells him out in bed. At the Table of the Lord he eats divinity,
devours God's flesh. He is insatiable, because the food that feeds
him incites him in his hunger....Fascinans! The divine obsession.
God beyond God calls to ineffable consummations. All among the
hay-stacks of the summer nights the Shulamite, Divine Wisdom,
enchants the soul.

— William Everson

POETRY AND HOLINESS GO TOGETHER, Everson tells us. Fascination, enchantment, instinct, and intelligence take hold of the
mystic and the poet. Divine wisdom enchants their souls and
inspires a "divine obsession." Have you ever felt the pull of a
divine obsession in your life? When have you let the mystic and
the poet emerge in you?

When I became a Catholic, not surprisingly, sex became divinized at a different level than it had been under Lawrence and the pantheistic aegis. As a pantheist, [I perceived that] sex was mostly instinctual and therefore closest to nature. It got its religious mode from that. But later on as a Catholic it emerged in its incarnational aspects. Traditionally, it has served as a metaphor of the love between God and man, as canonized in the Song of Songs, from Scripture. And for the most part, my program of erotic mysticism follows that vision. But then I brought the two strains together in River-Root, *probably my most important and revolutionary piece of writing. I fused the strains of Lawrence and Solomon together in an attempt to heal a division that has lain like a fracture in the sensibility of the race.*

— William Everson

EVERSON BELIEVES that there has been a division and a fracture in our species between sexuality and spirituality, so he set himself the task of laying out an "erotic mysticism." The religious element of sexuality, he believes, comes from primal natural instinct, but the spiritual dimension of incarnation and the role of Spirit comes from an awareness the Song of Songs gives us. What is your experience, and how would you describe the merging of sexuality and spirituality?

Catholicism gave me the mystical goal, the centering to touch the ecstasy. In pantheism there wasn't really enough focus to get that much ecstasy out of it....I often defended that move by calling it the barrel of the gun, the telescopic sight. The problem of pantheistic mysticism is its diffuseness.

— William Everson

PANTHEISM TEACHES that everything is God and God is everything. Panentheism teaches that all is in God and God is in all. Pantheism leaves out the transcendence or freedom and even the mystery or "beyondness" of Divinity. It limits Divinity to what is. Panentheism makes room for what is not, even for the black holes of the universe, and even perhaps for other universes. Everson believes that pantheism is too diffuse, too lacking in focus and centeredness. The Cosmic Christ teaching makes personal the cosmic panentheism, giving it a name, one might say. It localizes and renders intimate the divine, panentheistic presence.

[The erotic in mysticism] inheres in the scale of the American land-scape. The tension, the strain in the archetype exposes the unconscious, and the erotic root of the psyche is release from its collective repression and begins to sing. The erotic images sing spontaneously forward to match the equation between the contesting scales of psyche and landscape. The European landscape is more assimilable to cultural recourse, and therefore the erotic is more social conformist, whereas the American erotic component is more primal, the libido itself more animal oriented. Thus the American Indian models his fertility rites on the mating of the beasts he regarded as his ancestors.

— William Everson

EVERSON BELIEVES that the vastness and wildness of the American landscape give us insight about the wildness of the erotic. The Native American's closeness to nature and to wild animals also encourages that kind of connection. European consciousness has less of that wildness still intact. Do you agree with Everson? Is the wild a part of your sense of mysticism and of sexuality and the mergence of the two?

Faith is certitude in existence. I think mysticism professes this. It is the mystic's faith which enables him to transcend quotidian consciousness.... The prophet takes over where the mystic stops. The mystic is ascent; the prophet is descent.

— William Everson

DOES YOUR FAITH DEVELOP as a "certitude in existence"? Do you sense that trust is a deep part of your abiding mysticism? American philosopher William Hocking declared that the "prophet is the mystic in action" and the prophet, as we saw above, "interferes" (Rabbi Heschel). The mystic says Yes to life and the prophet says No to injustice and whatever interferes with life. The mystic encounters the Divine, ascending the mountaintop, but the prophet descends and returns to the dirty work of implementing the revelation of divine compassion. Does the prophet in you take over from the mystic in you?

Before the Pill the primacy of procreation in the sex life was so over-whelming that it had to be repressed, placed under taboo, strictly confined to the married state with enforced ignorance of its dynamic mechanism, because of the problem of responsibility for the fate of children. The sex act could only be implied in legitimate expression. The explicit was confined to the pornographic and sold under the counter. With the invention of contraception in the modern world the taboo was softened and we began to get fairly explicit renditions, but there was nothing like amnesty. Not until the invention of the Pill was mankind's apprehension sufficiently relaxed to feel safe with spontaneity.

— William Everson

HERE EVERSON puts our modern-day interest in sexuality in the cultural and historical context of the Pill and how it altered attitudes toward sexuality. Feeling "safe with spontaneity" seems to be something that developed only recently. Do you feel he is correct, and that attitudes toward sexuality have indeed evolved since the invention of the Pill?

The other thing about River-Root *is the religious dimension, or rather, the synthesis between sexual explicitness and religious awe, essentially regarding chastity. As long as sexual explicitness was confined to the obscene, religious awe was rigorously excluded from its presentation.... What* River-Root *did was to exercise the mental need for explicitness with religious awe that was the gift of chastity. The* Song of Songs *was the model historically, but the factor of explicitness was not yet achieved.*

The Song of Songs *is not a descriptive work; it's a chant; whereas* River-Root *is almost clinical in its description, though I set it in a religious context, which protects it from the excoriation of the profane.*

— William Everson

EVERSON BELIEVES HIS POEM on sexuality, set in a religious context, protected the explicit sexuality from mere profanity or pornography. He moved beyond obscenity because he was able to synthesize sexual explicitness with religious awe. What was your reaction to the poem? How important is it that we create such a synthesis in our sexuality?

It is important to recapture sexuality as a source of eschatology today because it's the most fulfilling experience. It is the most fulfilling because it centers the entire libido, the very life-drive, which in its highest registration is love, on the core of the soul's quintessence — man and woman, fused in ecstasy, the first magnitude of consciousness.

— William Everson

EVERSON BELIEVES LOVE and lovemaking constitute "the first magnitude of consciousness," and when tied to spirituality, they are the "most fulfilling experience." Is that your experience also?

It is natural that man should concern himself with beginnings. This is a part of the curiosity of the mind. Without it there would be no exploration of the world and there would be no growth.... This is an inherent characteristic of mind; it is not unique to any particular age of man, culture, or society. Contemplation concerning origins is a part of the curiosity of the race.

— Howard Thurman

THURMAN UNDERSCORES our inherent need for cosmology — the "curiosity of the race" includes curiosity about our origins, our beginnings, where we come from and where we find ourselves in the universe. All this is cosmology. We ought to be concerned with "beginnings"; these questions fuel our growth. How often do you wonder about these questions? Is it something you gave up at the end of your childhood? Today science is gifting us with a new story of the universe, one that is being understood around the world. We are also learning how our ancestors all came from Africa. A rebirth of wonder follows those who keep their curiosity about origins alive.

Jesus of Nazareth. To some he is the grand prototype of all the distilled longing of mankind for fulfillment, for wholeness, for perfection. To some he is the Eternal Presence hovering over all the myriad needs of humanity, yielding healing for the sick of body and soul, giving a lift to those whom weariness has overtaken in the long march, and calling out hidden purposes of destiny which are the common heritage.

To some he is more than a Presence; he is the God fact, the Divine Moment in human sin and human misery. To still others he is a man who found the answer to life's riddle, and out of a profound gratitude he becomes the Man most worthy of honor and praise.... Thus interpreted, he belongs to no age, no race, no creed. When men look into his face, they see etched the glory of their own possibilities, and their hearts whisper, "Thank you and thank God!"

— Howard Thurman

Do you understand Jesus as a "grand prototype" of the longings of human beings for fulfillment? Or as an "Eternal Presence" offering healing to the sick?

Do you see Jesus as a presence? As a God fact? As a divine moment in human misery? Do you see him as a person who found an answer to life's riddle? Do you see in his face the glory of your own possibilities? Do you agree that Jesus does not belong to any age, race, or creed? What are the implications of that?

What, then, is the word of the religion of Jesus to those who stand with their backs against the wall? There must be the clearest possible understanding of the anatomy of the issues facing them. They must recognize fear, deception, hatred, each for what it is. Once having done this, they must learn how to destroy these or to render themselves immune to their domination. In so great an undertaking it will become increasingly clear that the contradictions of life are not ultimate.

— Howard Thurman

THURMAN SEES JESUS as supportive of those who are oppressed and standing with "their backs against the wall." He says such people have to look fear and deception and hatred squarely in the eye and become immune to them. No denial! Have you undergone such awareness? Since we can't escape fear, deception, and hatred, what are ways we can avoid being controlled by them?

The disinherited will know for themselves that there is a Spirit at work in life and in the hearts of men which is committed to overcoming the world. It is universal, knowing no age, no race, no culture and no condition of men. For the privileged and the under privileged alike, if the individual puts at the disposal of the Spirit the needful dedication and discipline, he can live effectively in the chaos of the present the high destiny of a son of God.

— Howard Thurman

THURMAN BELIEVES we can live the "high destiny" of a son or daughter of God in the real world. He believes that the Spirit that teaches us the way is universal, and not subject to any age or race or culture. We can achieve this if we put ourselves "at the disposal of the Spirit" and commit ourselves to dedication and discipline. Have you made such a commitment, and do you feel yourself on a universal path of high destiny?

The evildoer does not go unpunished.
Life is its own restraint. In the wide sweep of the ebb and flow
of moral law our deeds track us down, and doer and deed meet.

— Howard Thurman

THURMAN IS SPEAKING OF KARMA, the law that we reap what we sow. Is this your belief also? Do you believe that our moral deeds "track us down"? This differs from the idea of an avenging and punitive Father in the sky who prepares a place for us in the fiery pits of hell. But it does, in a gentle way, urge us to take our choices seriously and our responsibility seriously.

The core of the analysis of Jesus is that man is a child of God, the God of life that sustains all of nature and guarantees all the intricacies of the life-process itself. Jesus suggests that it is quite unreasonable to assume that God, whose creative activity is expressed even in such details as the hairs of a man's head, would exclude from his concern the life, the vital spirit, of the man himself. This idea — that God is mindful of the individual — is of tremendous import in dealing with fear as a disease. In this world the socially disadvantaged man is constantly given a negative answer to the most important personal questions upon which mental health depends: "Who am I? What am I?"

— Howard Thurman

AS WE'VE SEEN, mystics often counsel us to lose our individual selves within the universal divine embrace. However, Thurman calls our attention to how this same embrace can bolster our individual sense of self in vital ways. Whenever human society dismisses us — whether because of our beliefs, gender, skin color, or gender preference — we can give in to fear and doubt ourselves, asking: Who am I? What am I? The teaching of Jesus, and the mystical understanding, that we are all children of the God of all life, can bolster us in these moments. We can and need to move from fear to self-acceptance. When have you felt the "disease" of fear threatening your mental health? How did you overcome this?

The awareness of being a child of God tends to stabilize the ego and results in a new courage, fearlessness, and power. I have seen it happen again and again.

When I was a youngster, this was drilled into me by my grandmother. The idea was given to her by a certain slave minister who, on occasion, held secret religious meetings with his fellow slaves. How everything in me quivered with the pulsing tremor of raw energy when, in her recital, she would come to the triumphant climax of the minister: "You — you are not niggers. You — you are not slaves. You are God's children." This established for them the ground of personal dignity, so that a profound sense of personal worth could absorb the fear reaction. This alone is not enough, but without it, nothing else is of value.

— Howard Thurman

THURMAN'S GRANDMOTHER, who lived with him when he grew up, was an ex-slave. She instructed him on many important issues, and this was one of his favorite and most telling stories. Moving beyond the internalized oppression of the oppressor to realizing his own God-likeness — this is where "courage, fearlessness, and power" arose in his soul. From this came "the ground of personal dignity" and a "profound sense of personal worth." How is your sense of personal dignity and personal worth these days? Like the preacher, do you work to inspire the same in others?

Precisely what does it mean to experience oneself as a human being? In the first place, it means that the individual must have a sense of kinship to life that transcends and goes beyond the immediate kinship of family or the organized kinship that binds him ethnically or racially or nationally. He has to feel that he belongs to his total environment. He has a sense of being an essential part of the structural relationship that exists between him and all other men and between him, all other men, and the total external environment. As a human being, then, he belongs to life and the whole kingdom of life that includes all that lives and perhaps, also, all that has ever lived. In other words, he sees himself as a part of a continuing breathing, living existence. To be a human being, then, is to be essentially alive in a living world.

— Howard Thurman

HERE, THURMAN DOESN'T ERASE INDIVIDUALISM but urges us, as all mystics do, to move beyond it. We must transcend our ethnic, racial, national, and familial identities to identify with the cosmos itself and all our relations. For as humans, "we belong to life and the whole kingdom of life" and the entire history of evolution that has brought us here. He personalizes cosmology in this passage. It strikes at an essential paradox: even though we are individual human beings, we must seek a "sense of kinship to life" that transcends all particulars. Can you also feel yourself swimming in the endless stream of the river of life?

*The profoundest disclosure in the religious experience is the aware-
ness that the individual is not alone. What he discovers as being true
and valid for himself must at last be a universal experience or else
it ultimately loses all of its personal significance. His experience is
personal, private, but in no sense exclusive. All of the vision of God
and holiness which he experiences, he must achieve in the context of
the social situation by which his day-by-day life is defined. What is
disclosed in this religious experience, he must define in community.*

— Howard Thurman

COMMUNITY IS AT THE HEART of Thurman's mysticism. What
we discover through our personal religious experience, we must
"define," or act upon, in community. Community becomes
the "test" as well as the beneficiary of our spiritual experience
— our experiences are "personal, private, but in no sense exclusive." And the profoundest revelation or disclosure we learn
through our religious experience is that "the individual is not
alone." What is true of our depths is true of others also. Indeed,
and again paradoxically, if we can't confirm that what we feel
is a "universal experience," we lose "all of its personal significance." What is deeply felt and learned about ourselves is a reflection of the depths of others. Have you felt this relationship
between self and community? Does each support the other?
Have you ever had your most private self be publicly recognized?

Jesus rests his case for the ultimate significance of life on the love ethic. Love is the intelligent, kindly but stern expression of kinship of one individual for another having as its purpose the maintenance and furtherance of life at its highest level....If we accept the basic proposition that life is one, arising out of a common center — God, all expressions of love are acts of God. Hate, then, becomes a form of annihilation of self and others; in short — suicide.

— Howard Thurman

THURMAN DESCRIBES A RADICAL KINSHIP, in which "all expressions of love are acts of God," and hate is the equivalent to murder or suicide. In other words, there are individuals, but there is no "other." Instead, "life is one, arising out of a common center," and that center is God. Love constitutes the "ultimate significance of life," and love carries us to life's "highest level." This is the essence of the teaching of Jesus. Do you feel this radical kinship? How can you help bring it to fruition?

The solution which Jesus found for himself and for Israel, as they faced the hostility of the Greco-Roman world, becomes the word and the work of redemption for all the cast-down people in every genera-tion and in every age. I mean this quite literally.... The basic fact is that Christianity as it was born in the mind of this Jewish teacher and thinker appears as a technique of survival for the oppressed. That it became, through the intervening years, a religion of the powerful and dominant, used sometimes as an instrument of oppression, must not tempt us into believing that it was thus in the mind and life of Jesus. "In him was life, and the life was the light of men." When-ever his spirit appears, the oppressed gather fresh courage; for he announced the good news that fear, hypocrisy, and hatred, the three hounds of hell that track the trail of the disinherited, need have no dominion over them.

— Howard Thurman

THURMAN'S READING OF HISTORY is that Christianity betrayed Jesus. In the mind of Jesus, the movement was a "technique of survival for the oppressed." Thurman distinguishes between what Jesus intended and what occurred historically when the Roman Empire married Christianity and subsequently a "reli-gion of the powerful and dominant" emerged, one sometimes used "as an instrument of oppression." In contrast, Jesus' spirit always gives "fresh courage" to the oppressed, and the good news he announced was that the "three hounds of hell" — fear, hypocrisy, and hatred — have no dominion over us. Do you agree with this distinction between Jesus' teachings and the church founded in his name? Do you believe fear, hypocrisy, and hatred can be overcome?

It is my belief that in the Presence of God there is neither male nor female, white nor black, Gentile nor Jew, Protestant nor Catholic, Hindu, Buddhist, nor Muslim, but a human spirit stripped to the literal substance of itself before God.

— Howard Thurman

HERE THURMAN is taking words from the writing of St. Paul and adding to them slightly. Both mystics are declaring that a radical equality exists between all people, whether male or female, Gentile or Jew; people of any faith or any race. This is part of the teaching of the kingdom of God that Jesus also preached, a kingdom of radical equality.

This teaching from Thurman carries special meaning in the twenty-first century, a time when, on the one hand, religious wars are being pronounced but, on the other hand, a new era of deep ecumenism and respect for the wonderful diversity of beliefs is also possible — and indeed necessary if we are to survive as a species. Do you agree with Paul and with Thurman? Do you sense a consciousness of equality coming into its own in our time?

Life is alive; this is its abiding quality as long as it prevails at all. The word "life" is synonymous with vitality.... We are so conscious of the fact of each individual expression of life about us that the simplest and most wonderful fact of all is passed by. And what is that? The fact that life itself is alive, has the persistent trait of living — that any and all living things continue to survive as long as that essential vitality is available to them.

— Howard Thurman

THURMAN SAYS we take for granted the "most wonderful fact of all" — the persistence of life itself. Life is *alive*! Do you take this for granted? How do we learn and teach one another not to take it for granted? How might our lives change if we rediscover this aliveness each day?

Man cannot long separate himself from nature without withering as a cut rose in a vase. One of the deceptive aspects of mind in man is to give him the illusion of being distinct from and over against but not a part of nature. It is but a single leap thus to regard nature as being so completely other than himself that he may exploit it, plunder it, and rape it with impunity.

— Howard Thurman

THURMAN GETS BEHIND THE SPIRITUAL MALAISE that has brought about the great devastation of the planet through ecological neglect. We have been living an illusion that we are not ourselves of nature but "distinct from and over against" nature — that we are here to "master" nature, as Francis Bacon and Descartes bragged about early in the modern age. The exploitation, plundering, and raping of nature have been the clear result.

Are you at home with your utter naturalness? Do you break with Bacon and Descartes and feel fully a part of nature? How do you live this? Do you demonstrate it at work, with family, in your citizenship, and in prayer?

This we see all around us in the modern world. Our atmosphere is polluted, our streams are poisoned, our hills are denuded, wild life is increasingly exterminated, while more and more man becomes an alien on the earth and fouler of his own nest. The price that is being exacted for this is a deep sense of isolation, of being rootless and a vagabond. Often I have surmised that this condition is more responsible for what seems to be the phenomenal increase in mental and emotional disturbances in modern life than the pressures — economic, social and political — that abound on every hand. The collective psyche shrieks with the agony that it feels as a part of the death cry of a pillaged nature.

— Howard Thurman

THURMAN MAKES CLEAR that even if humans feel alienated from nature, they nevertheless suffer along with it. As with hate, this is another form of "suicide," as humans become "part of the death cry of a pillaged nature." For Thurman, the ecological collapse is directly responsible for our modern spiritual crisis — "a deep sense of isolation, of being rootless and a vagabond." This, he believes, has more to do with the rise in mental and emotional illness in our society than do all other causes — economic, social, and political — put together.

What price do you feel we are paying for pillaging nature? Do you agree this is a spiritual crisis, and that we can heal our spirituality by renewing our kinship with the atmosphere, the land, and wildlife? How do we move from isolation and rootlessness to community and being at home?

Our own age seems primarily to need a rejuvenation of supernatural forces to be effected by driving roots deeply into the nutritious energies of the Earth. Because it is not sufficiently moved by a truly human compassion, because it is not exalted by a sufficiently passionate admiration of the universe, our religion is becoming enfeebled.

— Teilhard de Chardin

A JESUIT PRIEST AND SCIENTIST, Teilhard de Chardin proposes that "our religion is becoming enfeebled." We are too cut off from awe and wonder and a "passionate admiration of the universe." We are too anthropocentric, living our lives entirely in manufactured boxes. Thus we lack a "truly human compassion," and we are cut off from our deepest roots, which derive from "the nutritious energies of the Earth." Is religion enfeebled? How can we recover this sense of community and compassion and admiration?

Purity is not a debilitating separation from all created reality,
but an impulse carrying one through all forms of created beauty.

— Teilhard de Chardin

TEILHARD SEEKS TO REDEFINE "PURITY" from the ascetic tradition of cutting oneself off from that which is material and created and fleshy to being an instinct or an impulse that carries us through all forms of beauty. Purity for Teilhard is expansive, not restricted. So many forms reveal the divine beauty and to be pure is to pursue our inherent quest for beauty. Do you like this definition of purity? What is your definition of purity? What is the relationship between purity and beauty?

Till the very end of time matter will always remain young,
exuberant, sparkling, newborn for those who are willing.

— Teilhard de Chardin

TEILHARD SOUNDS VERY OPTIMISTIC HERE. He is not whining about how matter runs down and dies and renders us tired. Quite the opposite! He is saying that matter is always young and "will always remain young"; matter is always new. That is one of the spiritual insights derived from evolution and from observing life. Life, "matter," is constantly being created. But, as Teilhard points out, this perspective accrues only to "those who are willing." Individuals remain spiritually young when they are open and willing to join forces of youthfulness and renewal. Notice that evolution for Teilhard is not an obstacle to faith. Quite the opposite: it offers insight on the deeper dimensions of a spiritual life.

How young are we? Do we willingly and exuberantly embrace youthful change in life and history and evolution?

An ever increasing number of persons are beginning to distinguish a Noosphere which is like a halo around the biosphere....Noosphere... the living membrane which is stretched like a film over the lustrous surface of the star which holds us. An ultimate envelope taking on its own individuality and gradually detaching itself like a luminous aura, this envelope was not only conscious but thinking...the Very Soul of the Earth.

— Teilhard de Chardin

TEILHARD ATTEMPTS TO NAME "the Very Soul of the Earth." Today people are talking about Gaia, the earth as a living system. But decades ago Teilhard was also talking about the oneness of the earth and the "lustrous surface of the star which holds us," a halo or luminous envelope that protects us and is conscious and thinking. He called this the Noosphere.

What are the implications of this way of looking at the earth and the atmosphere?

Matter and Spirit: These were no longer two things but two states or two aspects of one and the same cosmic Stuff, according to whether it was looked at or carried further in the direction in which it is becoming itself or in the direction in which it is disintegrating. Matter is the Matrix of Spirit. Spirit is the higher state of Matter.

— Teilhard de Chardin

TEILHARD REDISCOVERED THIS ANCIENT TEACHING, which preceded the patriarchal teaching (rooted in Plato) of what Augustine called the "war" between matter and spirit, body and soul. Like Eckhart, who said "the soul loves the body," and like Aquinas, who taught that soul is the élan in matter, Teilhard celebrates the wonderful communion of matter and spirit. They are no longer "two things" but "two *states* or two aspects of one and the same cosmic Stuff." A marriage has occurred! Matter and spirit feed each other. Incarnation is not to be ignored. "Matter is the Matrix of Spirit" and "Spirit is a higher state of Matter."

When matter and spirit are wedded, what are the implications regarding our attitudes toward our bodies? Sexuality? Economics? Animals? The earth? Forms of education? Worship?

Matter was not ultra materialized as I would at first have believed, but was instead metamorphosed into Psyche. Spirit was by no means the enemy on the opposite pole of the Tangibility which it was seeking to attain: rather it was its very heart.

— Teilhard de Chardin

TEILHARD CAME TO REALIZE, by his study of evolution, that spirit was the "very heart" of matter, that matter evolved and morphed into psyche. Psyche was born of matter, and through all this evolving, spirit was present at the core of things. Teilhard invites us to be aware of consciousness everywhere and to recognize consciousness evolving. Spirit and tangibility are not enemies or even opposites.

Seek for the heart of tangible experience. Is that spirit at work for you also?

I give the name of cosmic sense to the more or less confused affinity that binds us psychologically to the All which envelops us. In order that the sense of humanity might emerge, it was necessary for civilization to begin to encircle the Earth. The cosmic sense must have been born as soon as humanity found itself facing the frost, the sea and the stars. And since then we find evidence of it in all our experience of the great and unbounded: in art, in poetry, and in religion.

— Teilhard de Chardin

TEILHARD TALKS OF "THE COSMIC SENSE" and how it came to evolve. He sees this cosmic awareness in all art, poetry, and religion worthy of the name, in "all our experience of the great and unbounded." This cosmic sense "binds us psychologically to the All which envelops us." This sense was awakened by the awesome awareness in humans of the sea and stars and frost. It is what is meant by the "Cosmic Christ," the presence of the divine image in all things that elicits awe from us.

Do you have this experience also? Do you express this through your art, poetry, and religion? How is our species doing today in expanding and expressing this cosmic sense? Do the Internet and the World Wide Web, for example, carry on this evolutionary trend?

Creatures can come into being like shoots from a stem,
only as part of an endlessly renewed process of evolution.

— Teilhard de Chardin

WE — AND ALL CREATURES — are "part of an endlessly renewed process of evolution." Do you feel that you are part
of this caravan of life? That you and every being you meet
are part of a fourteen-billion-year journey? Does this help to
arouse your sense of the sacred? Does this make you feel less
alone, less alienated, more alive, more enthused?

That magic word "evolution" which haunted my thoughts like a tune: which was to me like unsatisfied hunger, like a promise held out to me, like a summons to be answered.

— Teilhard de Chardin

TEILHARD FOUND POETRY and magic and music in the very word *evolution*. The promise, the summons he felt was to marry this scientific truth with spiritual truth, and he spent much of his life doing so. He also paid a dear price for doing so — most of his books were not published until after his death because the Catholic Church was threatened by his marriage of science, evolution, and religion.

What meaning does the word *evolution* carry for you? Is it a cold, objective, scientific fact, lacking wonder or spirit? Is it an unsettling challenge to religious beliefs, something to go to battle over? Can we see the joy, warmth, and magic that Teilhard found? What is evolution calling us to today? Are we generous enough to embrace it as a still-unsatisfied hunger?

To understand the world, knowledge is not enough.
You must see it, touch it, live in its presence and drink
the vital heat of existence in the very heart of reality.

— Teilhard de Chardin

TEILHARD URGES US TO MOVE beyond knowledge. Knowledge is not enough. We must taste life and make it very personal and erotic and unforgettable. Interestingly, the word for "wisdom" in both Hebrew and Latin derives from the word for "taste." "Taste and see that God is good" sings the Psalmist. Teilhard, too, is inviting us beyond knowledge to wisdom, and for wisdom to occur, we must taste life in all its dimensions — "see it, touch it, live in its presence and drink the vital heat of existence." In what ways are you drinking the vital heat of existence? In what ways would you like to?

Let us advance one step further. What name should we give to this physio-moral energy of personalization to which all activities displayed by the stuff of the universe are finally reduced? Only one name is possible, if we are to credit it with the generality and power that it should assume in rising to the cosmic order: love…. *The conclusion is always the same: Love is the most powerful and still the most unknown energy of the world.*

— Teilhard de Chardin

TEILHARD PLACES LOVE in the context of not just the personal and psychological but cosmology. He sees love, the "physio-moral energy of personalization," abounding in the universe. Have you made this shift also? What are some implications of this change of consciousness around the word *love*? How does it affect our experience of falling in love? And of religion itself?

Here the cosmic role of sexuality appears in its full breadth. And there at the same time, the rules appear which will guide us in the mastery of that terrifying energy in which the power that causes the universe to converge on itself passes through us.

The first of these rules is that love, in conformity with the general laws of creative union, contributes to the spiritual differentiations of the two beings which it brings together....

The one must not absorb the other nor, still less, should the two lose themselves in the enjoyments of physical possession, which would signify a lapse into plurality and return to nothingness.

— Teilhard de Chardin

SEXUALITY DWELLS IN A COSMIC CONTEXT — not just in a personal or ego or psychological one. Do you experience a cosmic connection when you make love? Teilhard cautions that true human love is not about surrendering one's autonomy. That way lies a return to nothingness.

To rediscover the sacredness of lovemaking is also to lift the veil on the shadow side of sexuality — misuse of sex, such as rape, renders a cosmic-size rupture in the human soul. Sexual abuse as a child can haunt a person for decades, well into adulthood.

Love is an adventure and a conquest. It survives and develops like the universe itself only by perpetual discovery.

— Teilhard de Chardin

TEILHARD SEEMS TO BE SAYING THAT LOVE, like the universe, is a process of self-discovery and adaptation, a basic element of evolution. This means that neither we nor the world is ever "finished." What have you found in your own relationships? Does romantic love survive and develop "only by perpetual discovery"? Does a marriage? How do we maintain an attitude of perpetual discovery and keep curiosity alive in everything we do?

> *By virtue of the creation and, still more, of the Incarnation,*
> nothing *here below is* profane *for those who know how to see.*
>
> — Teilhard de Chardin

SOME THEOLOGIES ARE VERY BUSY separating the sacred from the profane. Teilhard believes there is no such distinction. Eckhart said, "Nature is grace," thus refusing to separate nature from grace and the profane from the sacred. Teilhard attributes awareness of the marriage of the profane and the sacred to the Incarnation — or the understanding that God is enfleshed in history and evolution. The Cosmic Christ is present in all events. Do you agree with Teilhard and Eckhart? What are further implications of this awareness?

The powers that we have released could not possibly be absorbed by the narrow system of individual or national units which the architects of the human Earth have hitherto used. The age of nations has passed. Now, unless we wish to perish we must shake off our old prejudices and build the Earth.

— Teilhard de Chardin

TEILHARD CALLS US TO MOVE BEYOND NATIONALISM and individual power trips. He warns us that we have entered a new era, one requiring an earth consciousness, not a national or tribal consciousness. He wrote this partly in response to the dropping of the atomic bomb, and he sensed new structures and strategies needed to absorb and steer the great powers humans had unleashed

Similarly, consider the crisis of global warming we face today. How do we handle such matters as a species, since individual countries do not contain their own waste? We are all interconnected. Carbon dioxide released in China or the United States affects plant, animal, and human life all around the globe.

Do you see signs that nationalism is giving way to a larger earth consciousness? Where are we making the most progress, and where are we still holding back?

Up until now, to adore has meant to prefer God to things by referring them to God and by sacrificing them to God.

Now adoration means the giving of our body and soul to creative activity, joining that activity to God to bring the world to fulfillment by effort and intellectual exploration.

— Teilhard de Chardin

TEILHARD SHIFTS THE MEANING OF ADORATION of God from offering sacrifices to generously awakening our creativity. This awakened creativity requires much effort, study, and learning. This is how we honor and worship Divinity — the sacrifice required is not of animals and other physical offerings but of the direction and discipline we apply to our creativity. Do you agree? In what ways do you offer adoration?

Do not forget that the value and interest of life is not so much to do conspicuous things (although we must have this ambition) as to do ordinary things with the perception of their enormous value. This, I think, is the mystic to come.

— Teilhard de Chardin

TEILHARD PROPOSES that "the mystic to come" is one who is doing ordinary things while aware of their "enormous value." I hear him here endorsing a simple lifestyle — but to do so with zeal and generosity, with ambition. Are we there yet? What is holding us back? Are you the mystic to come?

Over every living thing which is to spring up, to grow, to flower, to ripen during this day say again the words: This is my Body.

And over every death-force which awaits in readiness to corrode, to wither, to cut down, speak again your commanding words which express the supreme mystery of faith: This is my Blood.

— Teilhard de Chardin

TEILHARD IS APPLYING THE WORDS from the Christian liturgy taken from Jesus' Last Supper experience to our everyday experience. Every living thing is the body of Christ, a Cosmic Christ. It is all sacred, all holy.

Teilhard also applies the liturgy to the everyday experience of the shadow side of life: the corroding, withering, cutting down that death-forces bring about. Every such event is the blood of the Cosmic Christ being shed anew. It is all sacred, all holy.

Sexuality is part of our inheritance from the animals, and in human nature there is an instinctive urge to transcend the physical level of sexuality and realize it at a deeper psychological and spiritual level. Ultimately, sexuality is the energy of love in human nature, and this can never be satisfied at either the physical or the psychological level, but always seeks fulfillment in the depths of the spirit, where it encounters the source of love.

— Bede Griffiths

BENEDICTINE MONK BEDE GRIFFITHS understands sexuality as our search for love and depth of spirit — it is "ultimately… the energy of love in human nature." Do you see sexuality this way? What follows from this understanding of sexuality?

In a sense the whole creation can be seen as a "marriage" between matter and mind, nature and spirit, Prakriti *and* Purusha, *in Hindu terms, and every human marriage is a reflection of the cosmic union. In the biblical tradition the people of Israel were seen as the "bride" of Yahweh and the climax of Israel's history was to be the marriage of Israel, the people of God, with its God.*

— Bede Griffiths

BEDE GRIFFITHS CELEBRATES the "'marriage' between matter and mind, nature and spirit" and how "every human marriage is a reflection of the cosmic union." Sacred metaphors abound about such marriages, including that of God to human beings. Do you celebrate these marriages? How do you do so? Does our culture celebrate them? What do we gain by publicly recognizing them, and what holds us back?

At Pentecost the disciples were "filled with the Holy Spirit." They underwent a radical transformation. Something happened which transformed them from a group of weak and spiritless men into a community of believers who set out to change the world. This something was a mystical experience. It was a breakthrough beyond time and change, beyond the agony of suffering and death which they had experienced in the crucifixion, into the world of absolute reality, which was summed up for the Hebrew in the name of God. They experienced God; they "realized Brahman," as a Hindu would say, they "Knew the Self, the Spirit, the eternal Truth, dwelling in the heart."

— Bede Griffiths

BEDE GRIFFITHS CALLS PENTECOST a transformational happening. The something that transformed the disciples from being weak to being courageous was in fact "a mystical experience." This underscores how important and how practical mystical experiences are. A mystical experience of God, "a breakthrough beyond time and change," inspires change in the world that matters. Do mystical experiences still occur today? Have you ever felt radically transformed, so that you moved beyond your fear and were emboldened by a timeless courage?

All the Christian churches, Eastern and Western, have to turn to the religions of the East, to Hinduism, Buddhism, Taoism and the subtle blend of all these in Oriental culture, and to the deep intuitions of tribal religion in Africa and elsewhere, if they are to recover their balance and evolve an authentic form of religion which will answer to the needs of the modern world.

— Bede Griffiths

FOR BEDE GRIFFITHS DEEP ECUMENISM is not about making nice with other religions. It is about recovering a "balance" and evolving "an authentic form of religion" that will address today's needs. Eastern and indigenous religions, he feels, have so much to teach about balance and healthy forms of religion. What do you know about religions other than your own? What speaks to you from them?

We have to go beyond all these historical structures and recover the original Myth of Christianity, the living truth which was revealed in the New Testament. But this cannot be done by the Western mind alone. We have to open ourselves to the revelation of the divine mystery, which took place in Asia, in Hinduism and Buddhism, in Taoism, Confucianism and Shintoism. Nor can we neglect the intuitive wisdom of more primitive people, the Australian Aborigines, the Polynesian Islanders, the African Bushmen, the American Indians, the Eskimos. All over the world the supreme Spirit has left signs of his presence. The Christian mystery is the mystery of God's presence in Man, and we cannot neglect any sign of that presence.

— Bede Griffiths

HERE, GRIFFITHS EXPANDS more specifically on the scope of his deep ecumenism, which includes all the religions of the East and all the indigenous religions of the world. Do you agree that "all over the world the supreme Spirit has left signs of his presence"? Do you agree with Griffiths that "God's presence in Man" can be found everywhere, including in the Christian mystery?

Intuition cannot be produced. It has to be allowed to happen. But that is just what the rational mind cannot endure. It wants to control everything. It is not prepared to be silent, to be still, to allow things to happen. Of course, there is a passivity of inertia, but this is an "active passivity." It is what the Chinese call wu wei, action in in- action. It is a state of receptivity.

— Bede Griffiths

BEDE GRIFFITHS SPEAKS OUT about the power of stillness and of allowing things to happen. This way is an offense to the ratio- nal mind. It is a "state of receptivity." The via negativa teaches us these matters. There we learn letting go and letting be.

There is an activity of the mind which is grasping, achieving, dominating, but there is also an activity which is receptive, attentive, open to others. This is what we have to learn. The classical expression of this intuitive wisdom is to be found in the Tao Te Ching, which speaks of the Spirit of the Valley and the Mystic Female.

— Bede Griffiths

BEDE GRIFFITHS BELIEVES that the East is better at the via negativa, which allows things to be themselves, than is the hyperactive West. This "intuitive wisdom" has a feminine dimension to it. Griffiths is addressing patriarchy's failures. Do you sense a correctness in what he is proposing?

"To return to the root is repose." These are the principles which underlie the wisdom of the East, which the West has to discover and which China and the East have to recover if the world is to find its balance.

— Bede Griffiths

IN MODERN TIMES, says Bede Griffiths, we are out of balance because we have lost the healthy path of repose that leads to the root. The East used to excel at repose but today the East too is losing its balance. This imbalance is as true of China and other Asian nations as it is of Europe and America. Activism is a disease of modern peoples. Do you sense this same imbalance in yourself? In your culture? What are you doing to find balance again?

The limitations of Western science and democracy have become more and more evident. The disastrous effects of Western industrialism, physical, social and psychological, polluting the world and threatening to destroy it, are only too evident. But this is not an "accident" due to the misuse of science and technology; it is due to a fundamental defect in Western man.... The balance can only be restored when a meeting takes place between East and West. This meeting must take place at the deepest level of the human consciousness. It is an encounter ultimately between the two fundamental dimensions of human nature: the male and the female — the masculine, rational, active, dominating power of the mind, and the feminine, intuitive, passive and receptive power.

— Bede Griffiths

BEDE GRIFFITHS LAYS THE CAUSE of the world's current ecological collapse very much at the feet of the one-sided consciousness of Western man and our failure to incorporate feminine consciousness into our awareness. This "fundamental defect" is the first thing to fix to restore a much-needed balance. Do you agree that consciousness is more important than technology? Does it change your way of seeing the world and of finding new ways of working for ecological sustainability?

The Church today consists of innumerable sects, each claiming to represent the true faith and denouncing the others as "heretical." The ecumenical movement has come to seek to overcome these divisions and to return to the unity of the Church, but unless it abandons the search for doctrinal formulas and legal systems, and recovers the intuitive wisdom of the Bible and of ancient man, there is little hope of success.

— Bede Griffiths

WHILE ACKNOWLEDGING THE NEED FOR ECUMENISM as both interfaith and intrafaith, Bede Griffiths offers a very sobering analysis: all of it is for naught if the emphasis is on doctrine and systems. The key to renewing the church today is "the intuitive wisdom of the Bible and of ancient man." This is a challenge to all the churches, all faiths, all doctrines. Do you see intuitive wisdom affecting your faith tradition and efforts at ecumenism? What can we do about incorporating more of the mystical and intuitive traditions into deep ecumenism?

It is here that the encounter with Eastern thought with its intuitive basis is crucial. Christianity cannot grow as a religion today, unless it abandons its Western culture with its rational understanding of the East. The suppression of women in the Church is but one of the many signs of this masculine domination.... Reason has to be "married" to intuition; it has to learn to surrender itself for the deeper intuitions of the spirit. These intuitions come, as we have seen, from the presence of the Spirit in the depths of the soul.

— Bede Griffiths

FOR BEDE GRIFFITHS, the "suppression of women in the Church" is the external manifestation of the defective, masculine-dominated consciousness that hobbles the West. Indeed, he says Christianity must "abandon its Western culture." Strong words. Where and how does this get fixed? It occurs when reason is "married" to intuition through encounters with the Spirit "in the depths of the soul." In other words, not only priests and bishops but everyone in the church must work for change. Does your church embrace this idea? Have you undergone such encounters, such breakthroughs and transformations?

The reunion of the Christian churches can only come, therefore, through a rediscovery of the "mystery of Christ" in all its dimensions, and this means that it must be related to the whole history of humanity and of the creation.... The narrow-mindedness which has divided the Christian churches from one another, has also divided the Christian religion from other religions. Today we have to open ourselves to the truth in all religions.

— Bede Griffiths

THE CALL TO "OPEN OURSELVES to the truth in all religions" is an attitude of deep ecumenism. Moreover, Griffiths implies that "narrow-minded" Christianity has lost its sense of the " 'mystery of Christ' in all it dimensions." Until this can be rediscovered, there will be no reunion of the churches. In other words, the Cosmic Christ needs to be rediscovered, for this relates to the "whole history of humanity and of the creation." How might we open ourselves to the truth in all religions?

Mahatma Gandhi himself was deeply influenced by the gospel, not only directly through the New Testament but still more indirectly through Ruskin and Tolstoy. Thus the social gospel of Christianity has come to be accepted in modern India and has been incorporated, one must say, into Hinduism. But in this process this social gospel has undergone a most significant transformation....

Gandhi has shown how the principles of the Sermon on the Mount can be applied to social and political life in a way which no one before him had done: he made the beatitudes a matter of practical concern in a way which few Christians have realized.

— Bede Griffiths

BEDE GRIFFITHS GIVES GANDHI CREDIT, and rightly so, for applying the principles of Jesus' teaching on the Sermon on the Mount to his work of nonviolence and his nonviolent overthrow of the British Empire in India. Griffiths also shows deep ecumenism at work: how to take what is useful and profound from the world's spiritual traditions and apply them. Sometimes this is a conscious, direct decision, but sometimes the influence is indirect; as Griffiths says, Gandhi encountered the Christian social gospel from writers such as Tolstoy, and in this roundabout way, Tolstoy also influenced modern Hinduism. As Griffiths says, few Christians have realized how to apply Jesus' teachings to real-life social change as Gandhi did — and Gandhi was not a Christian! Why do you think that is? Martin Luther King Jr. would be an exception, however.

Between the extremes of individual ownership to be found in capitalism and of collective ownership to be found in communism the Christian ideal is surely that of a co-operative society. Such a society allows a great deal of flexibility in methods of ownership, but it is firmly based on the principle of non-violence. It consists in the willing co-operation of free men, who spontaneously renounce their rights of ownership in order to work together for the common good. This was the idea which was once realized in the early Church and . . . it still remains a type of the Christian ideal.

— Bede Griffiths

BEDE GRIFFITHS PRESENTS the Christian "co-operative society" as a middle way between the extremes of capitalism and communism. This society depends on nonviolence and the "willing co-operation of free men," who will surrender ownership "in order to work for the common good." This ideal, Bede believes, was at the heart of the early church and to some degree still remains. In light of current economic woes and the financial rip-offs and fiascos of Wall Street, do you agree? Is this still an achievable ideal to strive for?

The whole Hindu temple is a shrine of this inner Spirit. The outer walls may be decorated with figures of animals and men and gods, so that one is led by stages through the different levels of life in this world, but in the central shrine — the garbha griha, representing the "cave of the heart" — there may be nothing but a lingam, a bare stone representing the formless divinity, the absolute godhead which is beyond all "name and form."

— Bede Griffiths

GRIFFITHS LIKED TO TALK of the "cave of the heart," and here he comments on its use in the sacred architecture of Hinduism. The outer temple begins where we usually being — with the outer world of creation — animals, men, even the gods. But the journey inward takes us to the center, and at the very cave of the heart we might find a representation of divine sacred sexuality — namely, the lingam, or a bare stone that represents not anything but the "formless divinity" and "absolute godhead," which is beyond all names, all metaphors, all forms.

How are we doing in our journey into the cave of our hearts? What do we find there? Is there space for the nothingness and unnameability of the Godhead? Is there a space for divine sacred sexuality? The void, or the divine womb, empty yet potentially all things?

The sexual origin of the lingam is, of course, obvious, but this only brings out the extraordinary depth of understanding in ancient India. Sex was always regarded as something "holy" — I think that it still is, except where the Indian spirit has been corrupted by the West. The lingam was therefore a natural symbol of the sacred "source of life."... The natural reaction of a European is to think that this is something "obscene"; but to me it seemed a touching expression of the sense of the sacred, the awareness of the essential holiness of nature and of faith in her generative powers.

— Bede Griffiths

"A TOUCHING EXPRESSION of the sense of the sacred" is how Griffiths understands the deep meaning of the lingam in the sacred architecture of the Hindu temples in India. This ancient culture has not separated sexuality from spirituality, as so many religions in the West have done. Bede observes how religion has distorted itself in the West when it regards sex as anything but holy. He challenges us — as does William Everson and others — to move beyond that mistake and act of "corruption."

Perhaps this is the deepest impression left by life in India, the sense of the sacred as something pervading the whole order of nature. Every hill and tree and river is holy, and the simplest human acts of eating and drinking, still more of birth and marriage, have all retained their sacred character.... In the West everything has become "profane"; it has been deliberately emptied of all religious meaning.... It is there that the West needs to learn from the East the sense of the "holy," of a transcendent mystery which is immanent in everything and which gives an ultimate meaning to life....

The Western world must recover this ancient vision of the three dimensions of reality. Then everything is sacred. That is what one finds in India; everything is sacred — eating or drinking or taking a bath; in any of the normal events of life there is always a sacred action.... We have lost that awareness.... [There is] this sacramentality of the universe. The whole creation is pervaded by God.

— Bede Griffiths

ACCORDING TO BEDE GRIFFITHS, what Westerners most need to learn from India is the "sense of the sacred" that pervades "the whole order of nature." This is creation spirituality, indeed. "Every hill and tree and river is holy" and the simplest human acts are also. We in the West have emptied the daily of all religious meaning. Is Bede accurate in his criticism of the West? In what ways has religious meaning been "emptied" from daily life in our Western culture?

Bede recognizes a "sacramentality of the universe," which everything that exists and all our daily actions are part of. This is what Teilhard de Chardin was also speaking about. How can we deepen our understanding and experience of the sacred in all things and all our daily actions? How can we create rituals that accomplish this?

The divine essence, the Holy Trinity, is totally present in every particle of matter, every atom, and every electron. However you would like to divine the universe, the whole creation is totally pervaded by God. The cosmic religion has this awareness of God pervading the whole creation which we, as a whole, have lost. The Hindu is still aware of the Divine Immanence in the universe.

— Bede Griffiths

AGAIN, LIKE TEILHARD, Bede sees God in "every particle of matter, every atom, and every electron." This is the Cosmic Christ tradition, the image of God in all things. Where does God exist for you? Can you spend a day breathing, touching, tasting, hearing, seeing the Divine in everything that exists, in everything you do?

In all these [religious] systems the danger is that the logical structure and rational doctrine will obscure the mystical vision, so inherent is the tendency of the rational mind to seek to dominate the truth which it should serve. This is the danger of all religion. It begins with a mystical experience, the experience of the seers of the Upanishads, of the Buddha under the bo tree, of the Hebrew prophets and the apostles at Pentecost, of Mahomet receiving the message of the Koran. But this experience has to be put into words; it has to descend into the outer world and take the forms of human speech. Already at this stage it is open to misinterpretation; the conflict between the letter and the spirit begins. Then the logical and rational mind comes and creates systems of thought: heresies and sects spring up, and the Truth is divided. This is due to the defect of the rational mind, imposing its narrow concepts and categories on the universal truth. Yet it cannot be avoided because the Truth must be proclaimed.

— Bede Griffiths

HERE GRIFFITHS DESCRIBES the distinction or split between spirituality and religion; this split is dangerous, yet it "cannot be avoided." The divine mystical experience is beyond words, yet humans have a seemingly intrinsic desire to explain, a need to proclaim the truth. But the moment we put the experience into words, we start to fight over the words: "the conflict between the letter and the spirit begins." There is a "defect of the rational mind" that robs the universal truth of its authenticity — and, we might add, that sells its soul readily to powerful forces of militarism, nationalism, and so forth. A kind of idolatry takes over.

How can we prevent this? How can we be on our toes to see this inherent danger of the rational mind? How can we preserve and honor mystical experience as the primary, universal truth?

The Truth has to be communicated and this cannot be done without words, which both express and veil the Truth. All sacred scriptures, the Vedas, the Buddhist Sutras, the Bible, the Koran, are subject to this law. They betray the Truth which they proclaim.

In each religion it is necessary to go back beyond its formulations, whether in scripture or tradition, to the original inspiration. . . . One must receive the Spirit by which the scriptures were inspired; one must be initiated into the Truth.

— Bede Griffiths

IN HIS CHARACTERISTICALLY STRONG LANGUAGE, Bede declares that "all sacred scriptures...betray the Truth which they proclaim." This warning means we cannot rely on words alone, even holy words from holy books, to understand divine truth. We have to "receive the Spirit" that inspired the scriptures in the first place. In other words, spiritual experience is necessary; each individual must be "initiated into the Truth" by journeying to the place beyond words. This is the true path to religious renewal. Have you taken this journey? How often? Does your religious community encourage this? Is there more you can do?

Western man has been turning outwards to the world of the senses for centuries and losing himself in outer space. He has to learn again to turn inwards and find his Self. He has to learn to explore not outer space but the inner space within the heart, to make that long and difficult journey to the Centre, to the inner depth and height of being, which Dante described in The Divine Comedy *compared with which the exploration of the moon and the other planets is the play of children.*

— Bede Griffiths

BEDE GRIFFITHS FEELS THE JOURNEY "to the Centre, to the inner depth and height of being" is vastly more important than our physical journeys to the stars. We have to "learn again to turn inwards and find his Self." Where is your focus — primarily inward or outward? Do you find the inner universe as exciting as outer space travel? Is it as full of beauty and surprises?

Each man must therefore discover this Centre in himself, this Ground of his being, this Law of his life. It is hidden in the depths of every soul, waiting to be discovered. It is the treasure hidden in a field, the pearl of great price. It is the one thing which is necessary, which can satisfy all our desires and answer all our needs....It is the original paradise from which we have all come.

— Bede Griffiths

WHAT IS IT THAT WE ARE LOOKING FOR when we turn inside? "It is the original paradise from which we have all come." It is the divine Source and origin of our being; it is "the pearl of great price," the kingdom of God within us. For all the wonders and pleasures of the world, only this, Bede says, "can satisfy all our desires and answer all our needs." How are we doing? How can we assist one another on this powerful and important journey?

The Buddha, Krishna, Christ — each is a unique revelation of God, of the divine Mystery, and each has to be understood in its historical context in its own peculiar mode of thought. To say that God is a person is not necessarily to deny that he is impersonal.... The Christian concept of God often becomes so personal that it needs to be corrected by the impersonalism of Buddhism.... To insist too much on the moral character of God can narrow our conception and lose something of that spontaneous freedom, that ecstasy of joy, which is found in Krishna.

— Bede Griffiths

BEDE GRIFFITHS CELEBRATES Buddha and Krishna — as well as Christ — as "a unique revelation of God." The particular cultural and historical contexts of these revelations help to balance the different dimensions of these incarnations. Taken together, they help us conceptualize what have been called divine paradoxes: God is both personal and impersonal.

God holds out moral challenges but also "spontaneous freedom" and joyful ecstasy. Religions have so much to learn from one another. Do you experience both personal and impersonal aspects of God? Does your spiritual journey include both ethical choices and ecstatic celebration?

*In Jesus myth and history meet. Myth reveals the ultimate meaning
and significance of life but it has no hold on history and loses itself in the world of imagination. History of itself, as mere succession
of events, has no meaning.... When historical events are seen to reveal the ultimate significance of life, then myth and history meet....
Man discovers his real nature and knows himself as a son of God.
The divine and the human meet "without separation and without
confusion."*

— Bede Griffiths

HERE BEDE GRIFFITHS SHEDS LIGHT on the stories of the New
Testament that have so captured the imagination of people because they tap into deep archetypes. Think of Christmas and its
many images — the animals at the manger, the stars leading the
Magi, the announcement to the shepherds. "In Jesus myth and
history meet." The Jesus story unleashed many mythical stories
such as these that cannot be denied for they speak deeply to the
human heart and the human condition.

But history also counts in the Jesus story: His taking on the
imperial powers of Rome through his preaching of the kingdom of God in contrast to the Roman Empire. How this led to
the historical event of his crucifixion. But Bede reminds us that
when myth and history meet, "man discovers his real nature
and knows himself as a son of God." This is where "the divine
and the human meet." This is incarnation. Does this ring true
to your experience? Can you live by history alone? Or by myth
alone? How do we combine the two?

All religion derives from a mystical experience, transcending thought, and seeks to express this experience, to give it form, in language, ritual, and social organization. Myth is the language of primitive religion: it is the poetic expression of a mystical experience. Myths can only be understood as poetry. They spring from the depths where man encounters the ultimate mystery of existence and interprets it in poetic form.

— Bede Griffiths

BEDE GRIFFITHS VALIDATES "primitive," or indigenous, religious myths as the equivalent to all other sacred spiritual understandings. They are all poetic attempts to articulate and proclaim mystical experience, "the depths where man encounters the ultimate mystery of existence." He also recognizes "language, ritual, and social organization" as types of poetic forms to "express this experience."

If this is true, then does it not follow that to renew religion is to return to mystical experience and to alter forms of language, ritual, and social organization accordingly? To invite the poetry out of people's hearts and the poet into the heart of religious education? So often religion, instead of renewing itself this way, defensively re-entrenches its social organization, makes walls of orthodoxy ever thicker, deepens slight differences into moats. Meanwhile, poetry withers, becomes ever distant. How is your religious tradition doing in this regard?

How can I get to know myself? Not by thinking, for thinking only reflects my conscious being, but by meditating. Meditation goes beyond the conscious mind into the unconscious. In meditation I can become aware of the ground of my being in matter, in life, in human consciousness. I can experience my solidarity with the universe, with the remotest star in outer space and with the minutest particle in the atom. I can experience my solidarity with every living thing, with the earth, with these flowers and coconut trees, with the birds and squirrels, with every human being. I can get beyond all these outer forms of things in time and space and discover the Ground from which they all spring. I can know the Father, the Origin, the Source, beyond being and non-being, the One "without a second." I can know the birth of all things from this Ground, their coming into being in the Word.

— Bede Griffiths

NOT SURPRISINGLY, Bede invites us to move from the act of thinking, which keeps us in the conscious mode, to meditating, which takes us "beyond the conscious mind" to a deeper place. He also tells us what we find in meditation: the ground of our being, our solidarity with all living beings, and the full breadth of the universe, from the stars to the particles within atoms. Only in wordless meditation can we move past duality, "beyond being and non-being," to the Origin, the Source, "the birth of all things." That's quite a benefit, wouldn't you say, to enter these realms of depth and relationship? Do you, or can you, make this a regular practice?

The central idea of the Eastern Fathers was that of theosis, *the divinization of all creatures, the transfiguration of the world, the idea of the cosmos and not the idea of personal salvation.... Only later Christian consciousness began to value the idea of hell more than the idea of the transfiguration and divinization of the world.... The kingdom of God is the transfiguration of the world, universal resurrection, a new heaven and a new earth.*

— Nicolas Berdyaev

THE IDEA THAT THE KINGDOM OF GOD is about life after death or about being saved from hell is an affront to the theology of Russian Orthodoxy, which is Berdyaev's tradition. Eastern Christianity teaches that individual salvation is not the point of the teaching of Jesus. (This was St. Augustine's idea more than a value in the Gospels.) Rather, theosis — "the divinization of all creatures, the transfiguration of the world" — is the central idea in the preaching of the kingdom of God by Jesus.

How does this alter your understanding of the message of Jesus? How are we doing in bringing about "a new heaven and a new earth" based on justice and compassion?

The greatest error of which historical Christianity is guilty is due to the circumscribing and deadening notion that revelation is finished and that there is nothing more to be expected, that the structure of the Church has been completely built and that the roof has been put on it. Religious controversy is essentially concerned with the problem of the possibility of a new revelation and of a new spiritual era. All other questions are of secondary importance.... The revelation of the Spirit cannot be just simply waited for; it depends also upon the creative activity of man; it cannot be understood simply as a new revelation of God to man; it is also a revelation of man to God. This means that it will be a divine-human revelation.

— Nicolas Berdyaev

BERDYAEV INSISTS THAT THE HOLY SPIRIT is not dead and all pooped out from writing the scriptures two thousand years ago. Rather, revelation is ongoing, and all things are in evolution, including church structures. Is there new revelation? Is there a "new spiritual era"? Berdyaev insists there must be. God waits for humans to be creative enough to bring about new insight, new forms, and new directions.

This echoes Bede Griffiths, Meister Eckhart, Teilhard de Chardin, and others who insist that divine revelation must be directly experienced now, in this moment, to be understood. Do you agree? Do you regard revelation as finished or constant? Are you waiting for God or searching for God or birthing God?

The greatest religious and moral truth to which man must grow is that we cannot be saved individually. My salvation presupposes the salvation of others also, the salvation of my neighbor, it presupposes universal salvation, the salvation of the whole world, the transfiguration of the world. The very idea of salvation arises from the oppressed condition of man; and it is associated with a forensic conception of Christianity. This ought to be replaced by the idea of creative transformation and enlightenment, by the idea of perfecting all life. "Behold I make all things new." It is not only God Who makes all things new, it is man too.

— Nicolas Berdyaev

BERDYAEV TAKES ON ST. AUGUSTINE and certain Western thinkers who think in terms of individual salvation. Salvation is communal; it involves not just myself but my neighbor and "the whole world." Further, humanity itself has a purpose beyond itself. Humanity is meant to be an active participant in the "creative transformation and enlightenment" that results in the "transfiguration of the world." We are destined to "make all things new," as God does.

You can tell the people that if they proceed in killing me, that I forgive and bless those who do it. Hopefully, they will realize that they are wasting their time. A bishop will die, but the church of God, which is the people, will never perish.

The church would betray its own love for God and its fidelity to the gospel if it stopped being a defender of the rights of the poor, or a humanizer of every legitimate struggle to achieve a more just society ... that prepares the way for the true reign of God in history.

When the church hears the cry of the oppressed it cannot but denounce the social structures that give rise to and perpetuate the misery from which the cry arises.

— Archbishop Oscar Romero

ROMERO PREDICTED HIS OWN MURDER, for this speech was given shortly before he was shot down while celebrating the liturgy. Around the same time, he wrote the American president begging him to cease providing money for the Salvadorian military, which was making war on the country's citizens. He stood for those with very little voice. He understood the church "is the people," more than it is structure or hierarchy. He walked his talk and paid the price of martyrdom. Do we continue to take courage from his example?

Blessed saint francis
pray for us
now and in the time of despondency
your brother the water is poisoned
children no longer know your brother the fire
the birds shun us

They belittle you
popes and czars
and the Americans buy up Assisi
including you
blessed saint francis
why did you come among us?

In the stony outskirts of the city
I saw you scurrying about
a dog pawing through garbage
even children
choose a plastic car
over you

— Dorothee Soelle

THE POET LAMENTS the breakdown in the ecosystem of our time and how it is an affront to all that Saint Francis stood for. She rages at the domination of those who reduce beauty to financial investment and buy up Francis's home town of Assisi. Do you share her concern and her outrage? What do you do with your anger and your moral disappointment?

Blessed saint francis
what have you changed
whom have you helped
Blessed saint francis
pray for us
now and when the rivers run dry
now and when our breath fails us.

— Dorothee Soelle

DOROTHY SOELLE ASKS PRIMAL QUESTIONS: Has Francis changed anything at all by his witness to Gospel values? Whom has he truly helped? We need his intercession before all the rivers run dry and before our polluted air so poisons us that our breathing fails. The criticism includes us, however: we have sentimentalized Francis and sucked his true prophetic spirit away from the moral ecological task at hand. How can we de-sentimentalize Francis and save him from a "bird bath" iconography?

If I'm absolutely still
I can hear the surge of the sea
from my bed
but it isn't enough to be absolutely still
I also have to draw my thoughts away from the land

It isn't enough to draw one's thoughts away from the land
I also have to attune my breathing to the sea
because I hear less when I breathe in

It isn't enough to attune one's breath to the sea
I also have to ban impatience from my hands and feet

It isn't enough to calm hands and feet
I also have to give up images

It isn't enough to give up images
I have to rid myself of striving

It isn't enough to be rid of striving
if I don't relinquish my ego

It isn't enough to relinquish the ego
I'm learning to fall

It isn't enough to fall
but as I fall
and drop away from myself
I no longer
seek the sea
because the sea
has come from the coast now

has entered my room
surrounds me

If I'm absolutely still.

— Dorothee Soelle

SOELLE DESCRIBES for us the letting-go process of the via negativa. This leads to the place beyond words that Bede Griffiths
describes. The letting go is endless. But it takes us to profound
places. Soelle promises us that as we learn to cease striving and
be still the sea itself will come to us and surround us. All distance is traversed. All dualism ceases. Oneing occurs. Have you
experienced this oneing yourself? How does it feel?

CREDO

I believe in god
who did not create an immutable world
a thing incapable of change
who does not govern according to eternal laws
that remain inviolate
or according to a natural order
of rich and poor
of the expert and the ignorant
of rulers and subjects
I believe in god
who willed conflict in life
and wanted us to change the status quo
through our work
through our politics

— Dorothee Soelle

SOELLE CALLS THIS POEM "CREDO." This is her belief, her creed, her understanding of Jesus' message and that of the Gospels. Soelle describes her God as one who works to "change the status quo," especially when that status quo supports dualisms of rich and poor, smart and dumb, ruler and subject. Her God does not govern by unchanging "eternal laws" but instead created conflict so that humans would work for change. Does this poetic reversal, in which God sowed conflict for our benefit, get at an underlying truth? How would your credo begin?

I believe in jesus christ
who was right when he
like each of us
just another individual who couldn't beat city hall
worked to change the status quo
and was destroyed
looking at him I see
how our intelligence is crippled
our imagination stifled
our efforts wasted
because we do not live as he did

— Dorothee Soelle

FOR SOELLE, Jesus was an average individual — one who worked to change the status quo but who could not beat city hall and was destroyed. For Soelle, Jesus' crucifixion was a very political act on the part of the empire and religious establishment that killed him. She calls us to "live as he did," and with that our imaginations will flourish. In your credo, what would be your understanding of Jesus?

every day I am afraid
that he died in vain
because he is buried in our churches
because we have betrayed his revolution
in our obedience to authority
and our fear of it
I believe in jesus christ
who rises again and again in our lives
so that we will be free
from prejudice and arrogance
from fear and hate
and carry on his revolution
and make way for his kingdom

— Dorothee Soelle

SOELLE LAMENTS what has happened to Jesus' revolution. She is afraid on a daily basis that he might have died in vain, for he is buried and his life betrayed. How? By our obedience to and fear of authority. Her belief is that his resurrection is ongoing in our lives, not a past event, and this will one day empty us of fear, hate, arrogance. Thus would his kingdom be born. Do you fear for Jesus' revolution, and how would you describe it working today?

I believe in the spirit
That jesus brought into the world
In the brotherhood of all nations
I believe it is up to us
What our earth becomes
A valley of tears starvation and tyranny
Or a city of god
I believe in a just peace
That can be achieved in the possibility of a meaningful life
For all people
I believe this world of god's
Has a future

Amen

— Dorothee Soelle

SOELLE CLOSES HER POEM "CREDO" with an affirmation and a word of hope. We humans can choose between a "valley of tears starvation and tyranny" or a "city of god" based on a just peace and a meaningful life for all. Our world has a future in such a God-like context. Do you share her hope? What would such a transformative meaningful life look like? How are you working toward realizing it?

When He Came

He needs you
That's all there is to it
Without you he's left hanging
Goes up in dachau's smoke
Is sugar and spice in the baker's hands
gets revalued in the next stock market crash
he's consumed and blown away
used up
without you

Help him
that's what faith is
he can't bring it about
his kingdom
couldn't then couldn't later can't now
not at any rate without you
and that is his irresistible appeal

— Dorothee Soelle

SOELLE RETURNS TO HER BELIEF IN JESUS: He is needy. He needs us to accomplish the work of compassion. "That's all there is to it." Otherwise the death camps return; he goes up "in dachau's smoke." He is part of what blows up when stock markets crash — unless we participate in redefining finance and economics. "Help him / that's what faith is." Faith is an action, a participatory action. Jesus dead or alive cannot do it without us. No kingdom without our work — never was, never will be. And that, for Soelle, is "his irresistible appeal."

Do you find this belief irresistible also? Do you believe that Jesus needs you, or that you need Jesus? What requires more faith: believing in his message or that his message can't live without you?

The goal of the Christian religion is not the idolizing of Christ, not christolatry, but that we all "are in Christ," as the mystical expression goes, that we have a part in the life of Christ. This savior is a wounded healer, and he heals so that we may become as he is. Be as he is, laugh as he laughs, weep as he weeps. Heal the sick, even those who without knowing it have contracted the great neuroses of our society, who know no mercy within themselves and their children when they consent to the nuclear state and technologies inimical to life. To feed the hungry means to do away with militarism. To bless the children means to leave the trees standing for them.

— Dorothee Soelle

SOELLE WARNS US ABOUT "CHRISTOLATRY," a certain form of idolatry. She argues instead for a mystical understanding of Christ, namely to be "in Christ," to share in the life of Christ and to heal, laugh, and weep as he did. We bless the children by leaving "trees standing for them." Mysticism heals religion when religion goes off target and becomes unbalanced and idolatrous.

Christolatry is the opposite of what it means to be "in Christ." Soren Kierkegaard practiced this distinction between those who esteem Christ and those who follow him. If I esteem him then I lift him ever higher and have nothing to do with him; I use my admiration to keep myself free of Christ. He is big, I am dependent on him, yet I do not want to go his way. But if I try to follow him, ... "Come along," he says, and that above all, "Come along into God's kingdom — to our home country, where no one is beaten, no one is thrown out and shoved away. Look and see," he says to me and show how the lame begin to walk. He does not say, "close your eyes; I'll do everything."

— Dorothee Soelle

SOELLE WARNS WHAT HAGIOGRAPHY can do to us: We put people (Jesus included) on pedestals often to get them out of our hair, so we don't have to change our lives or be bothered with their distant greatness. Following Christ is very different from idolizing him. It is doing what he did, healing and carrying on his work, since he cannot do everything. Is this your experience? Have you ever felt "safer" idolizing someone, seeing his or her greatness as beyond you? Can you replace that notion with the Christ of mysticism and be "in Christ"? The Christ of panentheism, Christological panentheism — we in Christ and Christ in us?

If Jesus of Nazareth was the poor man from Galilee who was tortured to death, then Christ is that which cannot be destroyed, which came into the world with him and lives through us in him. When I say Christ, I always think also of Francis of Assisi and Hildegard of Bingen and Martin Luther King, Jr. and of Ita Ford, the American nun who was murdered in El Salvador — as well as of all resistance fighters who are sitting in prison today. Christ is a name which for me expresses solidarity, hence suffering with, struggling with. Christ is the mysterious power which was in Jesus and which continues on and sometimes makes us into "fools in Christ," who without hope of success and without any objective, share life with others.

— Dorothee Soelle

SOELLE'S UNDERSTANDING OF CHRIST is that of the Cosmic Christ, the presence of the "mysterious power which was in Jesus" in all of us who struggle for justice and share solidarity with others in struggle. This work often renders us "fools in Christ." This Christ "lives through us in him," and this Christ inspires all the recent martyrs in his name, from Martin Luther King Jr. to Ita Ford, Oscar Romero, and Sister Dorothy, who was recently murdered in the Amazon for working on behalf of the rain forest and its peasant farmers. This is the Christ "which cannot be destroyed" and that rose from the dead after Good Friday. Do you experience this mysterious power in yourself and your work?

In feminist theology therefore, the issue is not about exchanging pronouns but about another way of thinking of transcendence. Transcendence is no longer to be understood as being independent of everything and ruling over everything else, but rather as being bound up in the web of life.... That means that we move from God-above-us to God-within-us and overcome false transcendence hierarchically conceived.

— Dorothee Soelle

SOELLE POINTS OUT that there is such a thing as "false transcendence" that derives from a "God-above-us" attitude. We can overcome it with a "God-within-us" perspective. Do you feel "bound up in the web of life"? This seems to echo what science tells us, that all things and all systems are interdependent. How different is this understanding of transcendence from that of rugged independence that rules "over everything else"? Is this kind of transcendence more about humble acceptance than ego-driven superiority?

We must approach mysticism, which comes closest to overcoming the hierarchical masculine concept of God — a mysticism to be sure, in which the thirst for real liberation does not lead to drowning in the sea of unconsciousness.... The mystical certainty that nothing can separate us from the love of God grows when we ourselves become one with love by placing ourselves, freely and without guarantee of success, on the side of love.

— Dorothee Soelle

SOELLE UNDERSTANDS A HEALTHY MYSTICISM to be the best antidote to a dangerous "masculine concept of God." A healthy mysticism leads to "real liberation," that is, to prophetic action. It does not wallow in a sea all by itself, drowning there in illusory incantations. The essence of the mystical experience is a "certainty that nothing can separate us from the love of God." This certainty builds courage and freedom and a willingness to love. How are we doing? Is this kind of mysticism alive and well in us and around us?

The language of religion, by which I do not mean the stolen language in which a male God ordains and imperial power radiates forth, is the language of mysticism: I am completely and utterly in God, I cannot fall out of God, I am imperishable. "Who shall separate us from the love of God?" we can then ask with Paul the mystic: "neither death nor life, height nor depth, neither present nor future" (Romans 8:35 and 38).

— Dorothee Soelle

SOELLE CRITICIZES THE LANGUAGE OF RELIGION — some of it is "stolen" and can be recognized because it is all male and echoes imperial power. The true language of religion is mysticism, and she defines this language as the realization that "I am completely and utterly in God, I cannot fall out of God, I am imperishable." This is strong language. Have you experienced this, that nothing whatsoever can separate you from the love of God?

I remember a feminist group in New York where we tried to speak of our own religious experiences. A woman...spoke about her sexual experience, which showed her for the first time what might be meant by the word "God" — that oceanic feeling of not being separate from anything or hindered by anything, the happiness of being one with everything living, the ecstasy in which the old "I" is abandoned and I am new and different.

— Dorothee Soelle

SOELLE, LIKE MALE AUTHORS such as William Everson, acknowledges that sexual love can be a profoundly mystical experience for women too. God is tasted in such acts of intimate sharing and in-depth lovemaking. Do you agree with Soelle and Everson? Is erotic mysticism alive and well?

Traditional psychological theory too soon runs out for the creative, the gifted, the deep woman. Traditional psychology is often spare or entirely silent about deeper issues important to women: the archetypal, the intuitive, the sexual and cyclical, the ages of women, a woman's way, a woman's knowing, her creative fire. This is what has driven my work on the Wild Woman archetype for the better part of two decades.

— Clarissa Pinkola Estés

CLARISSA PINKOLA ESTÉS SEEKS AN ARCHETYPE, what she calls the Wild Woman, that begins to name what is deepest in women: their creative fire, their ways of knowing, the intuitive. She believes that much of psychology has ignored that way of knowing and of being, and the creative, gifted, and deep woman does not get nourished by such a psychology. Do you agree that psychology needs to be deepened by the quest for the intuitive and creative fire or mysticism? Do you believe that psychology alone can adequately describe human potential and complexity?

Fairy tales, myths, and stories provide understandings which sharpen our sight so that we can pick out and pick up the path left by the wildish nature. The instruction found in story reassures us that the path has not run out, but still leads women deeper, and more deeply still, into their own knowing.... No matter by which culture a woman is influenced, she understands the words wild *and* woman, *intuitively.*

— Clarissa Pinkola Estés

STORIES AND MYTHS — the poetic language of the spirit — can lead to the inner knowledge we seek. Indeed, women of all cultures, Estés writes, recognize and understand "the words *wild* and *woman*, intuitively." When have you intuitively responded to archetypes or myths? What stories have instantly resonated in your soul? What does the archetype of the Wild Woman mean to you? Have you known women who practiced or embodied the attributes and talents you intuitively associate with it?

For some women, this vitalizing "taste of the wild" comes during pregnancy, during nursing their young, during the miracle of change in oneself as one raises a child, during attending to a love relationship as one would attend to a beloved garden.

A sense of her also comes through the vision; through sights of great beauty. I have felt her when I see what we call in the woodlands a Jesus-God sunset. I have felt her move in me from seeing the fishermen come up from the lake at dusk with lanterns lit, and also from seeing my newborn baby's toes all lined up like a row of sweet corn. We see her where we see her which is everywhere.

— Clarissa Pinkola Estés

DO YOU RESONATE with these examples of the "taste of the wild" that Estés names for us? That these are mystical experiences is clear when Estés says, "We see her…everywhere." Have you had similar experiences? What were they? What transformations in your life or work resulted from these experiences?

She comes to us through sound as well; through music which vibrates the sternum, excites the heart; it comes through the drum, the whistle, the call, and the cry. It comes through the written and the spoken word; sometimes a word, a sentence or a poem or a story, is so resonant, so right, it causes us to remember, at least for an instant, what substance we are really made from, and where is our true home.

— Clarissa Pinkola Estés

ESTÉS TELLS US THAT THE WILD WOMAN comes through music and through literature, as well as nature — through any creative expression that resonates so we remember our "true home." Is this your experience? Have you ever been so moved by music or poetry or writing that you experienced such a deep remembrance? Have you ever created something with the intention of awakening this in others? Estés honors the role of the artist in all of our lives, in ways that imagine the artist as a midwife of grace, the artist as priest.

The word wild *here is not used in its modern pejorative sense, meaning out of control, but in its original sense, which means to live a natural life — one in which the* criatura, creature, *has innate integrity and healthy boundaries. These words,* wild *and* woman, *cause women to remember who they are and what they are about. They create a metaphor to describe the force which funds all females. They personify a force that women cannot live without.*

— Clarissa Pinkola Estés

ESTÉS is describing a "force that women cannot live without." It's a metaphor that awakens women into remembering their divine source, which is "wild" because it's natural, not out of control. Do you resonate with that? Have you experienced such a force? Did it challenge you, change you?

The comprehension of this Wild Woman nature is not a religion but a practice. It is a psychology in its truest sense: a knowing of the soul.... When we lose touch with the instinctive psyche, we live in a semi-destroyed state and images and powers that are natural to the feminine are not allowed full development. When a woman is cut away from her basic source, she is sanitized, and her instincts and natural life cycles are lost, subsumed by the culture, or by the intellect or the ego — one's own or those belonging to others.

— Clarissa Pinkola Estés

BY DECLARING THAT GRASPING the Wild Woman's nature "is not a religion but a practice," I believe, Estés is saying that it is a spirituality and thus, in her words, "a knowing of the soul." Have you ever experienced the opposite, being cut off from your "basic source"? Do you know what it means to become "sanitized," to feel subsumed by the culture or the ego of others, or even of your own?

Wild Woman is the health of all women. Without her, women's psychology makes no sense.... When we understand the wildish nature as a being in its own right, one which animates and informs a woman's deepest life, then we can begin to develop in ways never thought possible. A psychology which fails to address this innate spiritual being at the center of feminine psychology fails women, and fails their daughters and their daughters' daughters far into all future matrilineal lines.

— Clarissa Pinkola Estés

ESTÉS SEEKS the "innate spiritual being at the center of feminine psychology" when she explores the Wild Woman, which is the "health of all women." This inner nature corresponds to a woman's "deepest life," allowing her to "develop in ways never thought possible." So much opens up. Have you contacted the innate spiritual being in you? How could you help our society's daughters access it?

To feel, think, or act in any of the following ways is to have partially severed or lost entirely the relationship with the deep instinctual psyche. Using women's language exclusively, these are: feeling extraordinarily dry, fatigued, frail, depressed, confused, gagged, muzzled, unaroused. Feeling frightened, halt or weak, without inspiration, without animation, without soulfulness, without meaning, shame-bearing, chronically fuming, volatile, stuck, uncreative, compressed, crazed, ... to be self-conscious, to be away from one's God or Gods, to be separated from one's revivification, drawn far into domesticity, intellectualism, work, or inertia because that is the safest place for one who has lost her instincts.

— Clarissa Pinkola Estés

ESTÉS NAMES WHAT HAPPENS TO US when we are cut off from our "deep instinctual psyche" — we fall into acedia, the lack of energy to begin new things (Aquinas). We become dry and depressed and we get set up for addictions — to domesticity, intellectualism, work, or inertia — which provide safe places to hide. Have you ever fallen into these or similar states? Was it hard to get out of them? What got you in touch with your deepest instinctual psyche again?

The archetype of the Wild Woman and all that stands behind her is patroness to all painters, writers, sculptors, dancers, thinkers, prayermakers, seekers, finders — for they are all busy with the work of invention, and that is the Wild Woman's main occupation. As in all art, she resides in the guts, not in the head.... She is the one who thunders after injustice.

— Clarissa Pinkola Estés

TO FIND THE WILD WOMAN INSIDE is to find the artist inside and to be busy with invention in all its possibilities. It is also to find the prophet inside, for she "thunders after injustice" — and that is what prophets do. Note that "she resides in the guts, not in the head." Finding her means traveling into our lower chakras, not living comfortably in our heads. The lower chakras are where our moral outrage resides and our sense of injustice is triggered, like a kick in the gut. Are you at home in your lower chakras? Is the prophet being nourished in you? Is the artist inside you being respected and released?

One of the most striking examples of loss of natural perception is in the generations of women whose mothers broke the tradition of teaching, preparing, and welcoming their daughters into the most basic and physical aspect of being women, menstruation. In our culture, but also in many others, the Devil changed the message so that first blood and all subsequent cycles of blood became surrounded with humiliation rather than wonder. This caused millions of young women to lose their inheritance of the miraculous body and instead to fear that they were dying, diseased, or being punished by God.

— Clarissa Pinkola Estés

ESTÉS CALLS OUR BODIES "miraculous." She decries the demonic culture that not only failed to guide young women through rites of passage to honor the sacredness of their physical evolution to adulthood but actually taught that blood cycles in young women were something to fear. This caused "humiliation rather than wonder."

What is your experience of puberty? Did anyone offer you something like a rite of passage to honor what was going on in your body? Did you feel wonder or humiliation about your body? What about others you know? Are we as a culture doing anything to alter this for subsequent generations of young people?

Three things differentiate living from the soul versus living from ego only. They are: the ability to sense and learn new ways; the tenacity to ride a rough road; and the patience to learn deep love over time. Raven-ego [in old stories, Raven is often portrayed as only liking bright, shining things, and neglecting to see the real treasure], however, has a penchant and proclivity to avoid learning. Patience is not ego's strong suit. Enduring in relationship is not Raven's forte. So it is not from the everchanging ego that we love another, but rather from the wild soul.

— Clarissa Pinkola Estés

ESTÉS CHALLENGES US to operate from the soul and not just from the ego. The latter guarantees that we are always learning "new ways," that we are tenacious and strong through difficult times, and that we undergo patience in learning to love over time. We love another "from the wild soul" and not from the ego that avoids learning and patience and endurance. How are we doing? Do we live more from the soul or more from the "Raven-ego"? How can we deepen our soul work and our soul-life?

"A wild patience," as poet Adrienne Rich puts it, *is required in order to untangle the bones, to learn the meaning of Lady Death, to have the tenacity to stay with her. It would be a mistake to think that it takes a muscle-bound hero to accomplish this. It does not. It takes a heart that is willing to die and be born and die and be born again and again.*

— Clarissa Pinkola Estés

TRUE COURAGE is not about gritting our teeth as a "muscle-bound hero" might do. True courage requires a "wild patience," and this derives from a heart "willing to die and be born" many times. How many times has your heart died and resurrected? How many times did your heart break but heal and move on? Do you harbor this wild patience?

*To be the keepers of the creative fire, and to have intimate knowing
about the Life/Death/Life cycles of all nature —
this is an initiated woman.*

— Clarissa Pinkola Estés

AN INITIATED WOMAN is one who is a keeper of the "creative fire." Are you such a person? Are you a keeper of the creative fire? If this means harboring intimate knowledge of the "Life/Death/Life cycles of all nature," are you such a person yet? Have you tasted this cosmic habit of life/death/life and seen it all around you in stars and leaves, animals and people? Are you able to share these mysteries with others? How do you prefer to go about this?

To create one must be able to respond. Creativity is the ability to respond to all that goes on around us, to choose from the hundreds of possibilities of thought, feeling, action and reaction — and to put these together in a unique response, expression, or message that carries moment, passion, and meaning. In this sense, loss of our creative milieu means finding ourselves limited to only one choice, divested of, suppressing, or censoring feelings and thoughts, not acting, not saying, doing, or being.

— Clarissa Pinkola Estés

ESTÉS EMPHASIZES THAT DIVERSITY and choice are necessary for creativity, which is above all a response "to all that goes on around us." How creative are you? Are you at home with diversity and choice? Is your milieu a creative one or is it a limited one that censors feelings, thoughts, and actions?

If we want to allow creativity its freedom, we have to allow our ideational lives to be let loose, to stream letting anything come, initially censoring nothing. That is creative life. It is made up of divine paradox. To create one must be willing to be stone stupid, to sit upon a throne on top of a jackass and spill rubies from one's mouth. Then the river will flow, then we can stand in the stream of its raining down. We can put out our skirts and shirts to catch as much as we can carry.

— Clarissa Pinkola Estés

CENSORING NOTHING, letting anything stream in, allowing our "ideational lives to be let loose" — these are Estés's ways of assuring we are living a creative life. How are we doing? Divine paradox is at the heart of creativity — laughter too. We can be fools and "stone stupid" and sitting on a jackass as on a throne. Have you done anything "stupid" lately? Anything stupid that brought bounty? Anything paradoxical? Is the river flowing yet? If not, why not?

Negative complexes are banished or transformed — your dreams will guide you the last part of the way — by putting your foot down, once and for all, and by saying, "I love my creative life more than I love cooperating with my own oppression."

— Clarissa Pinkola Estés

WE HAVE TO STAND UP — and put our foot down. We have to take a stand. We have to declare: "I love my creative life more than I love cooperating with my own oppression." That is when creativity begins. How are we doing? Have we chosen creativity yet? When was the last time you put your foot down to resist cooperating with your own oppression?

In myths and fairy tales, deities and other great spirits test the hearts of humans by showing up in various forms that disguise their divinity. They show up in robes, rags, silver sashes, or with muddy feet. They show up with skin dark as old wood, or in scales made of rose petal, as a frail child, as a lime-yellow old woman, as a man who cannot speak, or as an animal who can. The great powers are testing to see if humans have yet learned to recognize the greatness of soul in all its varying forms.

— Clarissa Pinkola Estés

THERE IS A "GREATNESS OF SOUL in all its varying forms," Estés insists. Have we experienced these marvels? Deities in rags? With muddy feet? As a frail child or an old woman? As a mute man or a talking animal? Where have we been hiding? Why are such stories and fairy tales so necessary to wake us up? Are they doing their job in our case?

The most valued lover, the most valuable parent, the most valued friend, the most valuable "wilderman," is the one who wishes to learn. Those who are not delighted by learning, those who cannot be enticed into new ideas or experiences, cannot develop past the roadpost they rest at now. If there is but one force which feeds the roots of pain, it is the refusal to learn beyond this moment.

— Clarissa Pinkola Estés

THE ONE FORCE feeding the very roots of pain is "the refusal to learn beyond this moment." The lack of curiosity. The smothering of curiosity, which is the instinct to learn. How are we doing? Are we among the most valued lovers, namely someone who is eager to always learn? Does anything keep us younger than an attitude of curiosity and learning?

The very idea of sexuality as sacred, and more specifically, obscenity as an aspect of sacred sexuality, is vital to the wildish nature. There were goddesses of obscenity (meaning regarding matters considered indecent by public measure) in the ancient women's cultures — so-called for their innocent (from the Latin, meaning "not harming") yet wily lewdness.... In fact, the dirty Goddesses represent that aspect of Wild Woman that is both sexual and sacred.

— Clarissa Pinkola Estés

ESTÉS, LIKE MANY TRULY MYSTICAL THINKERS we have examined, affirms the importance of the marriage of sexuality and spirituality. Obscenity is "an aspect of sacred sexuality" and is vital to our deepest nature. She differentiates between a sexuality decided by culture and sexuality as growth of spirit and soul. Can we bring erotic mysticism back? How are we doing?

Unless we affirm God as He who calls man into existence and to freedom and to love which is the fulfillment of that freedom — unless we affirm this God we fail to affirm that without which man's life has no meaning....In the conflict between law and freedom, God is on the side of freedom. That is a scandalous statement! But it is the New Testament! How are we going to affirm to the modern world the scandal of the New Testament? It is here that we confront the seriousness of our prophetic as distinct from our contemplative calling.

— Thomas Merton

THOMAS MERTON FEELS that only by affirming a God of freedom and love does human life have meaning. Further, when he says that ultimately "God is on the side of freedom," and not the law, he recognizes this is "scandalous" news. Yet it lies at the heart of New Testament teaching. What forms do freedom and love take for you? Are these central to the meaningfulness of your life, your work, your relationships? What are you doing to spread the scandal of freedom?

In the interior life there should be moments of relaxation, freedom and "browsing." Perhaps the best way to do this is in the midst of nature, but also in literature. Perhaps also a certain amount of art is necessary, and music.... You also need a good garden, and you need access to the woods, or to the sea. Get out in those hills and really be in the midst of nature a little bit! That is not only legitimate, it is in a certain way necessary.... The woods and nature should be part of your solitude, and if it's not periodically part of your solitude I think the law should be changed.

— Thomas Merton

HERE MERTON PROVIDES US with a prescription for healthy solitude. By definition it means separating yourself from human interaction for a time, but nature is a necessary part of your solitude. Music, art, and literature are also helpful and useful, but a garden, the woods, the sea, the hills — Merton feels these elements are essential to our deepest solitude.

Is that your experience? Is nature integral to your spiritual practice? Do you give yourself the time and space to allow nature to speak to you heart to heart? To listen to the Creator embedded there?

All through those weary first days in jail when I was in solitary confinement, the only thoughts that brought comfort to my soul were those lines in the Psalms that expressed the terror and misery of man suddenly stricken and abandoned. Solitude and hunger and weariness of spirit — these sharpened my perceptions so that I suffered not only my own sorrow but the sorrows of those about me. I was no longer myself. I was man. I was no longer a young girl, part of a radical movement seeking justice for those oppressed. I was the oppressed. I was that drug addict, screaming and tossing in her cell, beating her head against the wall. I was that shoplifter who for rebellion was sentenced to solitary. I was that woman who had killed her children, who had murdered her lover.

— Dorothy Day

DOROTHY DAY DESCRIBES the deep meaning of compassion. In prison, her consciousness expanded beyond her literal self; she identified with everyone around her, each sorrowing and in need. The via negativa of prison helped to empty her of ego so that she learned compassion in a deep way. Have you undergone similar experiences? What ways have you learned compassion?

The blackness of hell was all about me. The sorrows of the world encompassed me. I was like one gone down into the pit. Hope had forsaken me. I was the mother whose child had been raped and slain. I was the mother who had borne the monster who had done it. I was even that monster, feeling in my own heart every abomination.

— Dorothy Day

DAY'S EXPERIENCES of the via negativa in solitary confinement in jail led her into what felt like "the blackness of hell." Her sense of self disintegrated, such that she became one with every victim and every victimizer. This is where divine compassion ultimately leads, to our identification with all aspects of humanity. Thich Naht Hahn talks in very similar language about his experiences among the refugees and boat people of Vietnam. Have you had similar experiences?

We are not expecting utopia here on this earth. But God meant things to be much easier than we have made them. A man has a natural right to food, clothing and shelter. A certain amount of goods is necessary to lead a good life. A family needs work as well as bread. Property is proper to man. We must keep repeating these things. Eternal life begins now, "all the way to heaven is heaven, because He said, 'I am the Way.' " The Cross is there of course, but "in the Cross is joy of spirit." And love makes all things easy....

Love is indeed a harsh and dreadful thing to ask of us, of each of us, but it is the only answer.... To the saints everyone is child and lover. Everyone is Christ.

— Dorothy Day

DAY IS SPEAKING IN PARADOX, as so many mystics must. She says "love makes all things easy," and then she warns us love is "a harsh and dreadful thing." Is it both? Apparently so. Have you experienced both aspects of love? Day adds that we are all lovers and all other Christs. What follows from that awareness?

The contemplative life should liberate and purify the imagination which passively absorbs all kinds of things without our realizing it; liberate and purify it from the influence of so much violence done by the bombardment of social images. There is a kind of contagion that affects the imagination unconsciously much more than we realize. It emanates from things like advertisements and from all the spurious fantasies that are thrown at us by our commercial society. These fantasies are deliberately intended to exercise a powerful effect on our conscious and subconscious minds. They are directed right at our instincts and appetites and there is no question but that they exercise a real transforming power on our whole psychic structures. The contemplative life should liberate us from that kind of pressure, which is really a form of tyranny.

— Thomas Merton

THE ADVERTISING WORLD — so omnipresent and so powerful and seductive with its clever and artistic ways — can be a subtle form of tyranny, Merton observes. It deliberately and powerfully affects our conscious and subconscious minds. It gets inside and creates a "kind of contagion" on our imaginations. Nurturing a contemplative life helps purify our minds and imaginations of the "violence" we are bombarded with. This cleansing of "our instincts and appetites" is necessary because it is precisely our appetites and desires that advertisers seek to influence.

Have you developed a regular contemplative practice? Is it strong enough to diffuse, purify, and laugh at the commercial babble so intent on stealing our imaginations from us?

The strictly scientific view of the universe needs this dimension of love and play, which it sorely lacks. That is one thing I like about space flights: at last there is something of cosmic play getting into the somber, unimaginative, and superserious world of science. But what is a little play of astronauts against the great, gloomy, dogmatic seriousness of the death game, nuclear war? Can we recover from the titanic humorlessness of our civilization?

— Thomas Merton

DO YOU AGREE that our civilization is lacking in humor? That it dwells in a state of "titanic humorlessness"? Merton wants to balance the human, scientific quest for knowledge with Wisdom's quest for play and contemplation. He is warning us not to trust scientists who themselves cannot play. Do you share his thoughts? Is science without mirth? Is there room in a rational society for "cosmic play"?

Heisenberg's Physics and Philosophy *is a very exciting book. The uncertainty principle is oddly like St. John of the Cross. As God in the highest eludes the grasp of concepts, being pure Act, so the ultimate constitution of matter cannot be reduced to conceptual terms.* There is, logically speaking, nothing there that we can objectively know. *(Unless you want to use the abstract concept of pure potency, but what does it mean?)*

This seems to me to be the end of conventional nineteenth-century materialism — which, funnily enough, now appears exactly for what it was: a "faith," and not science at all. To be more precise, let us say a "myth," which was accepted on faith in the "authority of science."

— Thomas Merton

MERTON THE MONK, reading physicist Werner Heisenberg's famous book, finds it very exciting. He compares it to the great mystic John of the Cross — for both science and mysticism move beyond concepts. Matter is beyond conceptual grasping, as is God. Merton announces the death of nineteenth-century materialism, and a number of scientists such as Fritjof Capra, Rupert Sheldrake, and David Bohm have since said the same. As all these writers have shown, postmaterialistic, quantum science and spirituality and mysticism have much to teach and learn from one another. Are we listening? What good scientists have you read lately?

Martin Luther King, who is no fanatic but a true Christian, writes a damning letter from Birmingham jail, saying that the churches have utterly failed the Negro. In the end, that is what the Black Muslims are saying too. And there is truth in it. Not that there is not a certain amount of liberal and sincere concern for civil rights among Christians, even among ministers, priests, and bishops. But what is this sincerity worth? What does this "good will" amount to? Is it anything more than a spiritual luxury to calm the conscience of those who cultivate it? What good does it do the Negro? What good does it do the country? Is it a pure evasion of reality?

— Thomas Merton

MERTON WRITES during the heart of the civil rights revolution. He supports King, who was still then very controversial, but he also highlights the spiritual necessity of action. What good is conscience if it is not expressed in works? Merton makes clear that even sincere expressions of goodwill and concern on the part of Christians amounted to an "evasion of reality" if they didn't lead to participation in the movement to justice. What causes today call to our consciences to fight in the name of solidarity and justice?

I stepped out of the north wing of the monastery and looked out at the pasture where the calves usually are. It was empty of calves. Instead there was a small white colt, running beautifully up the hill, and down, and around again, with a long smooth stride and with the ease of flight. Yet in the middle of it he would break into rough, delightful cavorting, hurling himself sideways at the wind and the hill, and instantly sliding back into the smooth canter. How beautiful is life this spring!

— Thomas Merton

THE BEAUTY OF LIFE in springtime caught Merton's eye and soul — and it was a small white colt that did the bidding. Are we alert and ready for the small events that reawaken our sense of spring, our sense of life renewed? Of life living itself? Are we affected daily by the wonder that life bestows on us?

No art form stirs or moves me more deeply, perhaps, than Paleolithic cave painting — that and Byzantine or Russian icons. (I admit this may be really inconsistent!)

The cave painters were concerned not with composition, not with "beauty," but with the peculiar immediacy of the most direct vision. The bison they paint is not a mere representation of an animal, it is a sign, a gestalt, *a presence of the unique and peculiar life force incarnated in this animal — in terms of Bantu philosophy, its* muntu. *This is anything but an "abstract essence." It is dynamic power, vitality, the self-realization of life in act, something that flashes out in a split second, is seen, yet is not accessible to mere reflection, still less to analysis.*

Cave art is a sign of pure seeing, nothing else.

— Thomas Merton

IT IS INTERESTING TO LEARN that ancient cave paintings so moved Thomas Merton. He sees their work as disciplined and direct, like the work of contemplation itself — "pure seeing, nothing else." And in that seeing is a "dynamic power" and "vitality" that is not self-conscious but immediate. This reflection on ancient art seems to confirm how profound and important art is to our species as an expression of spiritual experiences. A "self-realization of life in act" is what is seen, and that is what is at stake in living fully in this world so full of wonders. Do you have such experiences regularly? Who or what helps to trigger them? Have we lost this art of unself-consciousness and immediacy? Can we find it again?

When psalms surprise me with their music
And antiphons turn to rum
The Spirit sings: the bottom drops out of my soul

And from the center of my cellar Love, louder than thunder
Opens a heave of naked air.

— Thomas Merton

THOMAS MERTON'S POEM about singing the psalms, which is a regular practice for the monk, tells us how exhilarating the experience can be. The songs "turn to rum," they intoxicate in delicious ways. "The Spirit sings" — not just the monks alone — and the "bottom drops out of my soul." That is, deep journeys down into the soul take place, and from that "cellar," the cellar of love, there "opens a heave of naked air." This is a beautiful way of talking about what happens to us when we pray deeply. Have you experienced such whole-body prayer, giving voice from the roots of your being? How did it transform you?

... The whole
World is secretly on fire. The stones
Burn, even the stones
They burn me. How can a man be still or
Listen to all things burning? How can he dare
To sit with them when
All their silence
Is on fire?

— Thomas Merton

MERTON SEES into the stones and how they, like the rest of creation, are on fire. He has learned this truth from sitting still and listening "to all things burning." He has learned this lesson from silence. Even the silence burns. The fire of stones speaks to his fire, for they burn him. This language of burning may be another way of speaking about encountering the Cosmic Christ, the light in all things. Light burns. To say the "whole world is secretly on fire" conjures up Moses' experience of God in the burning bush. Every bush is a burning bush — this we now know from today's science. Every bush, all matter, contains photons or light waves, which in theological language might represent the light in all things, that which burns in all things.

Are you burning also? Are you sitting still to experience the secret fire in all things? Merton warns that it takes daring.

Be still
Listen to the stones of the wall
Be silent, they try
To speak your

Name.
Listen
To the living walls.

Who are you?
Who
Are you? Whose
Silence are you?

— Thomas Merton

MERTON INVITES US TO LISTEN to the stones talking. This requires silence and attention. They are personal; they speak our name. The walls live. They ask us questions: "Who are you?" and "Whose silence are you?" The Bible speaks of the cornerstone of the wall that was rejected. In Christian terms, the Christ is that cornerstone. Is that stone speaking to us also? Is every being speaking to us if we dare to listen?

Of course it is true that religion on a superficial level, religion that is untrue to itself and to God, easily comes to serve as the "opium of the people." And this takes place whenever religion and prayer invoke the name of God for reasons and ends that have nothing to do with him. When religion becomes a mere artificial façade to justify a social or economic system — when religion hands over its rites and language completely to the political propagandist, and when prayer becomes the vehicle for a purely secular ideological program, then religion does tend to become an opiate. It deadens the spirit.... This brings about the alienation of the believer so that his religious zeal becomes political fanaticism. His faith in God, while preserving its traditional formulas, becomes in fact faith in his own nation, class or race. His ethic ceases to be the law of God and of love, and becomes the law that might-makes-right: established privilege justifies every-thing, God is the status quo.

— Thomas Merton

MERTON'S GOD OF FREEDOM is antithetical to God as the status quo. The latter, Merton warns, is dangerous, "a mere artificial façade to justify a social or economic system." What would be examples of that? When does religion deaden the spirit and reduce belief to political fanaticism? How do we guard our own faith from becoming reduced to faith in one's "own nation, class or race"?

One reason why our meditation never gets started is perhaps that we never make this real, serious return to the center of our own nothingness before God.... We do not begin by seeking to "find our heart," that is to sink into a deep awareness of the ground of our identity before God and in God.... [O]ur true self is not easy to find. It is hidden in obscurity and "nothingness," at the center where we are in direct dependence on God.

— Thomas Merton

MERTON REMINDS US that our "true self" — as distinct from our "false self," our external persona — is "not easy to find. It is hidden in obscurity." So how do we find that true self? Are we condemned to living superficial lives? We find the true self through meditation, Merton proposes, and by seeking to "find our heart" and sink into the ground of our "identity before God and in God." We also find it by encountering our "nothingness," which is also at the center of our God experience. Have you had experiences of your nothingness? Or do you shy away from it? Are you making that journey, sinking into "a deep awareness"?

All that has been said . . . of Christian mysticism about "dark contemplation" and "the night of sense" must not be misinterpreted to mean that the normal culture of the senses, of artistic taste, of imagination, and of intelligence should be formally renounced by anyone interested in a life of meditation and prayer. On the contrary, such culture is presupposed. One cannot go beyond what one has not yet attained, and normally the realization that God is "beyond images, symbols and ideas" dawns only on one who has previously made a good use of all these things.

— Thomas Merton

MERTON MAKES CLEAR there is no use or need for anti-intellectualism in the spiritual life. The via positiva precedes the via negativa; we need both. In fact, one leads directly to the other: the life of meditation and prayer that takes us into the via negativa and dark contemplation presupposes imagination, intelligence, artistic taste. The truth that God is "beyond images" usually comes to "one who has previously made a good use of all these things."

The function of image, symbol, poetry, music, chant, and of ritual (remotely related to sacred dance) is to open up the inner self to the contemplative to incorporate the senses and the body in the totality of the self-orientation to God that is necessary for worship and for meditation.

— Thomas Merton

MERTON CELEBRATES THE ROLE OF ART and artist in the contemplative journey. He proposes that art is not merely decorative or expressive but functional on this journey. All art, from image to music, from chant to ritual and dance, can play the role of opening up the inner self to both worship and meditation. The senses and the body are part of that awakening and opening.

Contemplation is essentially a listening in silence, an expectancy. And yet in a certain sense, we must truly begin to hear God when we have ceased to listen. What is the explanation of this paradox? Perhaps only that there is a higher kind of listening, which is not an attentiveness to some special wave length, a receptivity to a certain kind of message, but a general emptiness that waits to realize the fullness of the message of God within its own apparent void.

— Thomas Merton

MERTON EXPLORES THE VOID, the silence, the "general emptiness" that awaits the fulfilling message of God. Indeed, he defines contemplation here as "an expectancy." An advent. A waiting and "listening in silence." Listening comes in many forms, and listening to the silence and emptiness is one of them. Mindfulness derives from mind-emptiness.

How many people there are in the world of today who have "lost their faith" along with the vain hopes and illusions of their childhood. What they called "faith" was just one among all the other illusions. They placed all their hope in a certain sense of spiritual peace, of comfort, of interior equilibrium, of self-respect. Then when they began to struggle with the real difficulties and burdens of mature life, when they became aware of their own weakness, they lost their peace, they let go of their precious self-respect, and it became impossible for them to "believe."

— Thomas Merton

MERTON PROPOSES THAT OUR FAITH is often childish — not childlike but immature. Our faith in God may be more like faith in Santa Claus, and we think the spiritual life is meant to reward us with peace, comfort, inner equilibrium, and self-respect. But the via negativa comes, chaos ensues, and our certainty falters, breaks up. Struggling with "the real difficulties and burdens of mature life" and with the real choices that confront us, we lose our faith and feel we are on our own. Maybe, instead, we are just being baptized into the deeper realm of faith, the place where hearts break and worlds fall apart, the dark night of the soul. There is where our "preciousness" gets pierced through. There is where true trust or faith begins.

Place no hope in the feeling of assurance, in spiritual comfort. You may well have to get along without this. Place no hope in the inspirational preachers of Christian sunshine, who are able to pick you up and set you back on your feet and make you feel good for three or four days — until you fold up and collapse into despair.

Self-confidence is a precious natural gift, a sign of health. But it is not the same thing as faith. Faith is much deeper, and it must be deep enough to subsist when we are weak, when we are sick, when our self-confidence is gone, when our self-respect is gone.

— Thomas Merton

FAITH TAKES US TO DEEP PLACES, to the ruptures in our self-confidence and our lives. Do not settle for spiritual comfort all the time, for the "preachers of Christian sunshine." Darkness is divine also. Faith is not about positive thinking so much as about the perseverance that kicks in when we are weak, sick, and full of doubt. The via positiva never stands alone. The via negativa is always with us on our faith journey as well. Does this resonate with your experience?

Contemplation is the highest expression of man's intellectual and spiritual life. It is that life itself, fully awake, fully active, fully aware that it is alive. It is spiritual wonder. It is spontaneous awe at the sacredness of life, of being. It is gratitude for life, for awareness and for being. It is a vivid realization of the fact that life and being in us proceed from an invisible, transcendent and infinitely abundant Source. Contemplation is, above all, awareness of the reality of that Source.

— Thomas Merton

IN THIS DEFINITION OF CONTEMPLATION Merton stresses the aspect of the via positiva. It is the fullness of both our intellectual and spiritual life. It is life awake and alive and "fully aware that it is alive." It is awe and wonder and gratitude for being. It is a return to the source of all that wonder and being and an "awareness of the reality of that Source." Do you practice this divine contemplation, and balance it with action and engagement in the world?

We ourselves are "the Second Adam" because we ourselves are Christ. In us, the image of God, which is complete and entire in each individual soul, is also, in all of us "the image of God." The first Adam, "who is one man in all of us," is saved and transformed by the action of Christ and becomes, in us, the second Adam.... We see that we ourselves are Adam, we ourselves are Christ, and that we are all dwelling in one another, by virtue of the unity of the divine image reformed by grace.

— Thomas Merton

"WE OURSELVES ARE CHRIST." How many preachers and teachers and theologians have you heard speak this teaching? It is a deep mystical teaching that is too often neglected. Christ is not present exclusively in Jesus; Christ lives in all who walk the path of wisdom. We too are truly "the image of God." We are Christ, we are Adam, and "we are all dwelling in one another."

323.

Jesus not only teaches us the Christian life, He creates it in our souls by the action of His Spirit. Our life in Him is not a matter of mere ethical goodwill. It is not a mere moral perfection. It is an entirely new spiritual reality, an inner transformation.

— Thomas Merton

WHEN WE FIND CHRIST in ourselves, we go beyond ethics, beyond correct teachings, beyond moral duty and perfection. We embody "an entirely new spiritual reality, an inner transformation" that happens because Jesus "creates" something in us by the "action of His Spirit." Jesus both teaches and unleashes Spirit, which touches us and alters us even as we struggle to live ethical and moral lives. Spirit takes us deeper.

*When I was suddenly catapulted into the leadership of the bus pro-
test in Montgomery, Alabama, a few years ago, I felt we would be
supported by the white church. I felt that the white ministers, priests
and rabbis of the South would be among our strongest allies. Instead,
some have been outright opponents, refusing to understand the freedom movement and misrepresenting its leaders; all too many others
have been more cautious than courageous and have remained silent
behind the anesthetizing security of stained-glass windows.*

— Martin Luther King Jr.

MARTIN LUTHER KING JR. SPEAKS of his disappointment in the
South's white ministers, priests, and rabbis, his fellow religious
leaders. He felt they would help support the struggle for justice
in the civil rights revolution. Instead of courage he found cau-
tion; instead of support he found silence. Instead of pursuing
justice and embracing the God of freedom, many others hid all
wrapped up in "the anesthetizing security of stained-glass windows." Religion and religious symbols were used not to serve
authentic faith but to serve fear and preserve injustice.

This still happens in today's world, in ways large and
small. Is religion today in touch with its prophetic spirit? Does
religion speak out where and when it needs to?

In the midst of a mighty struggle to rid our nation of racial and economic injustice, I have heard many ministers say: "Those are social issues, with which the gospel has no real concern." And I have watched many churches commit themselves to a completely other-worldly religion which makes a strange, un-Biblical distinction between body and soul, between the sacred and the secular.

— Martin Luther King Jr.

NOTICE THAT KING'S DISAPPOINTMENT with ministers who claim that gospel is not concerned with social issues is fired by an awareness of the philosophy behind that morally lackadaisical attitude: the dualistic theology that separates body from soul and sacred from secular. To ignore the body is to ignore the body politic and the suffering in the body politic. King rightly points out that these dualisms are un-biblical.

In deep disappointment I have wept over the laxity of the church.... Yes, I love the church. How could I do otherwise?... Yes, I see the church as the body of Christ. But, oh! How we have blemished and scarred that body through social neglect and through fear of being nonconformists....

There was a time when the church was very powerful — in the time when the early Christians rejoiced at being deemed worthy to suffer for what they believed. In those days the church was not merely a thermometer that recorded the ideas and principles of popular opinion; it was a thermostat that transformed the mores of society.... Small in number, they were big in commitment. They were too God-intoxicated to be "astronomically intimidated."... Things are different now. So often the contemporary church is a weak, ineffectual voice with an uncertain sound. So often it is an archdefender of the status quo. Far from being disturbed by the presence of the church the power structure of the average community is consoled by the church's silent — and often even vocal — sanction of things as they are.

— Martin Luther King Jr.

KING WEEPS OVER THE FAILURES of the church. Do we also? What work of reformation of religion and church can we effectively bring about?

King longs for the courage of the early church when Christians stood up to the Roman Empire, even if that stance was dangerous and brought the wrath of the empire upon them. He saw a living church as one that transformed the mores of society. How much, if anything, has changed since King's day? To what degree do churches still defend the status quo and sanction things as they are?

But the judgment of God is upon the church as never before. If today's church does not recapture the sacrificial spirit of the early church, it will lose its authenticity, forfeit the loyalty of millions, and be dismissed as an irrelevant social club with no meaning for the twentieth century. Every day I meet young people whose disappointment with the church has turned into outright disgust.

— Martin Luther King Jr.

YOUNG PEOPLE, ESPECIALLY, YEARN for what is authentic, and they are keenly discerning when society and its institutions fall short. When the church protects the status quo — becoming a "social club with no meaning" — then it ceases to reflect "the sacrificial spirit of the early church." In what ways do young people today discover the sacrificial spirit in religion or other ways of service? Do you find that spirit more often outside or inside the church?

Is organized religion too inextricably bound to the status quo to save our nation and the world? Perhaps I must turn my faith to the inner spiritual church, the church within the church as the true ekklesia *and the hope of the world. But again I am thankful to God that some noble souls from the ranks of organized religion have broken loose from the paralyzing chains of conformity and joined us as active partners in the struggle for freedom. They have left their secure congregations and walked the streets of Albany, Georgia, with us.... Yes, they have gone to jail with us. Some have been dismissed from their churches, have lost the support of their bishops and fellow ministers.... Their witness has been the spiritual salt that has preserved the true meaning of the gospel in these troubled times.*

— Martin Luther King Jr.

SOMETIMES TO BE CHURCH you have to leave church or take on the acrimony of church leaders. Yet this witness provides the "spiritual salt" that puts meaning into Gospel values. Organized religion, when it's too beholden to society's status quo, forfeits its status as authentic church, and so King speaks of searching for an "inner spiritual church, the church within the church," that will carry authentic hope into the world. Have you ever felt this tension between organized religion and the inner spiritual church? How did you resolve it? Where did that journey take you?

The history of man, the history of the spirit is, by ontological necessity, tied up with the history of nature. For man is, in the full sense of the word, a microcosm. For that matter, even the sacred history of man is the story of an incarnation and not the history of angelic creatures! ... The corporality of the human being is the ontological foundation of his sociability. . . . Social individuality has no meaning with reference to a pure spirit. Mankind is a people: every individual is at the service of the species.

— M. D. Chenu

LIKE MARTIN LUTHER KING JR., Chenu decries the separation of body and spirit, of history and religion. Chenu insists that any history involving humans is a history of nature; even our religions are a "story of an incarnation," not a description of disembodied spirit. We are truly a microcosm of the macrocosm, a small mirror of the greater cosmos. Our very bodiliness is the basis for our sense of community and self. Each person "is at the service of the species," that is, the whole community, including nature and evolution. These are important distinctions, since religious ideologies that separate matter from spirit will also separate religion from social justice and will provide justification to those who would lord it over others because of their self-defined superiority.

History is made by the free acts of individuals and all moments of time but only through the sociability of man who lives in time. History is not a succession of biographies. . . . Social progress is characteristically the process whereby acts of interpersonal love become exteriorized in objective social justice.

— M. D. Chenu

INTERPERSONAL LOVE needs to find its fullest expression in social justice. Think of the work of Gandhi, Martin Luther King Jr., or Nelson Mandela, who opened the consciousness of so many both to injustice and also to ways (such as nonviolence) to end injustice. History is not about individuals so much as about the unfolding sociability of human beings, that is, the expansion of a justice consciousness. Love becomes justice, and this makes history happen, and in this way evolution advances over time.

If "capitalism" is simply a system based on profit so that the whole economic system is regulated by profit, then Christianity would demand the elimination of profit altogether.... We must understand that it is not excesses or abuses of various kinds which render this whole system undesirable and immoral.... Suppose that an enterprise begins with a capital of a million (francs) and after ten years has increased to five million: if these five million belong to the capital as such the fault is due not to the avarice of individuals but to the evil of the system.... A further fault of such a system is that the benefits are not used for the service of the common good. *This service is the necessary justification of every productive enterprise, because work always has a double role: it must first provide a personal benefit but it must ultimately be orientated toward community needs.*

— M. D. Chenu

IN OUR TIMES of colossal financial collapse and malfeasance on Wall Street, it is important to put things into moral perspective. Chenu makes the point that the greed of individuals is a symptom, not the cause. Any economic system that values only profit is evil; it's a system that rewards avarice, lying, and injustice. Regulation of such a system, to keep avarice and injustice under control, is certainly necessary, but Chenu goes further: A system based on profits alone requires Christians to stand up and "demand the elimination of profit altogether." The common good and community needs are key moral tests of any economic system, Chenu reminds us.

How are we doing? How is Wall Street doing? Do you experience this conflict between Christianity and the current version of capitalism? Is Main Street being violated by Wall Street? What would a "moral" economic system look like?

Inspired by converging evolutions our generation would seem to have the task of finally determining the human truth of matter in its historical dimension. For matter is impressing its importance in the many phases of man's collective life and in the psychological life of soul.... It is a daring assertion which proclaims the philosophical and religious truth of matter.... In the finest hour of the University of Paris, in the emancipated world of the Communes, Thomas Aquinas roused the anger and disdain of intellectuals and religious people by proclaiming the importance of matter in the metaphysics of the universe, in the constitution of man and in the evolution of society.

— M. D. Chenu

CHENU, A GREAT HISTORIAN, feels that history today is challenging us to look at matter differently. Science is discovering whole new dimensions in both the quantum world and the cosmic world. Yet our religious consciousness is often burdened with negative teachings about matter. Future generations will judge us on the stand we took about matter. Need matter and spirit be at odds? Do body and soul have to clash? Does spirituality have nothing important to say about work, lovemaking, economics, or ecology?

Chenu finds a historical precedent for the affirmation of the spiritual importance of matter in Aquinas, who dared to arouse opposition from both intellectuals and religious people in the thirteenth century by emphasizing the "importance of matter in the metaphysics of the universe, in the constitution of man and in the evolution of society." For this reason Aquinas was condemned after he died. Only later was he canonized. To value matter is to value those who study matter, scientists. The struggle that Aquinas waged with fundamentalists and dualists in his day is still going on with fundamentalists today.

Man is body and soul: matter enters into the definition of man. Matter is not something juxtaposed to an autonomous spirit and here again Marx is right against all forms of Cartesianism. Matter is not a fragile and compromising support for spirit, not a passing habitation in preparation for a definitive life. It is consubstantially "present" in man, and through it we can see the operations of the spirit.

— M. D. Chenu

IN ACADEMIC, INTELLECTUAL LANGUAGE, Chenu describes what earlier mystics such as Julian of Norwich proclaimed in more spiritual, metaphorical language: Matter does not drag spirit down, nor is it separate or distinct from spirit. Rather, "through [matter] we can see the operations of the spirit." The latent Platonism in Western religion and the spirit/matter split in Augustine's thinking are dangerous. They scapegoat matter as the source of evil. Such is not the case. Matter is inherent in human beings and in all the glory of creation. It is therefore "consubstantially 'present'" in us. We need to stand up for matter. That is what incarnation means. It is a privilege — not a burden — to be light incarnated as matter, which is what we truly are and what all the marvelous creatures of this planet are.

Nature is religious in its very essence. The star-studded firmament, for example, is one great supplication. The spirit of every landscape is a spirit of prayer, and so is the deep silence of solitary places.

The crickets and the stars speak to us of God, and what they are telling us is that they were created by God.

The entire cosmos aspires to a union with that God from whom it has gone forth.... The law of love is the supreme physical and biological law of the universe and also the one and only moral law ("I give you a new commandment: love one another as I have loved you").

— Ernesto Cardenal

CARDENAL INVITES US again into the religious life of nature. Stars and landscapes, crickets and the cosmos, are all testifying to the one "supreme physical and biological law of the universe...love one another." When have you experienced nature as "religious in its very essence"?

All the appetites and anxieties of man, his eating habits, his sexuality, his friendships, are one single appetite and one single anxiety to achieve union with one another and with the cosmos.... This cosmic homecoming is what Christ wanted to reveal to us in the parable of the Prodigal Son.

— Ernesto Cardenal

OUR APPETITES AND OUR ANXIETIES are all about achieving "union with one another and with the cosmos." This is the *unio mystica*, the mystical union. It is a "cosmic homecoming." We are all welcomed home just like the young man in the story of the prodigal son. Are you at home with this one, deep truth?

We have come from the heart of God
and are as much a part of him as the fetus is a part of the mother.
And we all tend to return to Him
as man tends to return to the maternal womb.

— Ernesto Cardenal

IN PROPOSING THAT WE ARE TO GOD as the fetus is to the mother, Cardenal is operating from a metaphor of God as mother. Many changes in our perception of Divinity flow from such a theology. In what ways, as adults, do we seek to return to that divine, maternal womb? Attending a sweat lodge is certainly one such experience. What other rituals accomplish that? How do other elements of theology change when we acknowledge the maternal side of Divinity?

All things have an element of enchantment but also an element of disenchantment and disappointment. The enchantment derives from the fact that all things are reflections and images of God, and the disenchantment is due to the fact that they are only images and not the real reality. They are not God.

— Ernesto Cardenal

HAVE YOU EXPERIENCED THE "ENCHANTMENT" of all things that Cardenal praises? Have you also experienced the "disenchantment" he names? The enchantment comes from the reflection of God that every image of God (which is every being) possesses. The disenchantment derives from the fact that things are images only and not the fullness of the divine reality. Here, Cardenal tracks the via positiva (enchantment) and the via negativa (disenchantment). We inevitably taste both along our spiritual way, don't we?

There is a paradox when we acknowledge the Divinity in things but also recognize the limits of Divinity in things. Fullness and nothingness both speak of the Divine.

Nothing in the universe is ugly. There is only beauty or a relative lack of beauty, a relative lack of the divine sheen in certain particular things.

Beauty, joy and pleasure appear in beings in a diluted form, but all things are nonetheless bathed in and illumined by beauty in varying degrees, as though overlaid with a diffuse light. God alone is Light in its purity; He is the focus of all that is lighted.

Things bear in themselves an element of beauty, beauty in greater or lesser degree, but they are not Beauty as such. God is the light that bathes all beautiful bodies, and there is nothing in Him that is not pure Beauty.

— Ernesto Cardenal

CARDENAL RETURNS TO THE PREMODERN TEACHING of Aquinas and Hildegard and Eckhart that God is beauty itself but that all beings carry their brand of the divine beauty imperfectly but for real. The light and beauty of the Cosmic Christ emanate from all beings. But no being is the fullness of the Cosmic Christ and the image of God.

Only by dying to ourselves do we encounter our true identity, because our true identity is not in our ego but in the All. We are centered in God as are all other things and beings.... Our ego is a solitary place, and he who rejects suffering and defies death and refuses to give himself, but wants to retain his self, shuts himself out of that Unity of all things which is God ("If the grain of wheat does not die, it remains alone...").

— Ernesto Cardenal

CARDENAL RECALLS THE UNIVERSAL CYCLE of living, dying, and being reborn. We cannot resist that cycle even before our earthly death. We undergo many deaths, and in the process become vulnerable to an experience of "the All." We fall like the grain into death, and in the process we spring to new life and new existence, just like the little shoot growing from the seed. Have you experienced the little deaths of self that lead to new life?

All sexual love is a symbol of divine love. As a matter of fact, every poet who celebrates his beloved in song, all the love poetry of the world, all human love and even the non-rational love of animals, the fertilization process of plants and the cohesive force of inert matter is a form and type of divine love.

Marriage has such enchantment and is something divine for us because it is an image of the divine espousal.

— Ernesto Cardenal

ALL LOVE "is a form and type of divine love." Whether we are speaking of lovemaking between humans, of expressions of love in song or poetry, or of any type of procreation within nature, it is all an expression of divine love at work in the universe. And marriage is profound because it too images "the divine espousal." It embodies the future of human and divine intercourse.

Maybe this is why gay and lesbian lovers the world over are seeking to have their unions acknowledged as marriage also. Maybe the struggle for gay marriage is a struggle to implement more fully the image of the divine espousal, a refreshing of the enchantment that marriage is meant to testify to.

In every human desire, in every human appetite, there is a great deal of energy, passion and fire. And this energy and this fire reach their greatest intensity when the soul wholly abandons itself, to desire henceforth only one thing and one love! ... Passions, appetites, affections, instincts and all the many anxieties of the human heart are the fuel of the love of God. Actually, the entire human being is this kind of fuel. And the love with which God responds to the soul may be compared with the pouring of oil on fire.

— Ernesto Cardenal

HUMAN DESIRE AND HUMAN APPETITES are not an obstacle to spirituality. Rather, the energy, passion, and fire they carry come to a special intensity when the soul lets go of little objects and seeks "only one thing and one love." Our passions are our "fuel" and indeed, "the entire human being is this kind of fuel." God's response is still more fuel, still more fire, still more love. That is how energy is recycled.

When we feel that a person we love requites our love, this intensifies our own love. Nothing, in fact, incites our love more than the knowledge that the beloved returns our love, and any increase of love on the part of the beloved intensifies in turn the love that burns in ourselves.

— Ernesto Cardenal

WHEN ANOTHER SAYS YES TO OUR LOVE and returns it to us, love doubles and triples in its presence and intensity. Love begets love. Love births love. The burning deepens and goes on and on.

God is eternally young and new. His works are always vernal, and the world is reborn every morning at daybreak as though it had just been created.

The dawn of every day is a new "Let there be light!" and has the freshness and novelty of that first dawn. God makes the elderly leap joyfully in the early morning, and He causes the doves to frolic and the mockingbirds to sing of that God "who is the joy of my youth."…His is the only love that never ages, and He is the only love who is neither unfaithful nor mortal.

— Ernesto Cardenal

THE WORLD IS BORN NEW EVERY DAY. The declaration "Let there be light!" is renewed with each sunrise. Does it change your morning to think of creation itself as something ongoing and happening again, right now? God is the "joy of my youth" — do you feel that youthfulness on a regular basis? Do you feel that God's love never ages and is never unfaithful and does not die?

*Prayer is as natural to man as speaking, sighing and seeing,
as natural as the palpitation of a loving heart; and actually that is
what prayer is: a murmur, a sigh, a glance, a heartbeat of love.*

— Ernesto Cardenal

WHAT IS YOUR DEFINITION OF PRAYER? Would it include "a murmur, a sigh, a glance, a heartbeat of love"? Is prayer only set phrases to be read from a book, or listening to someone else repeat those phrases on our behalf? Or is it "as natural... as speaking, sighing and seeing"? Cardenal is saying that any acknowledgment or expression of love is prayer. If prayer has become a dull, rote exercise in devotion, it may be necessary to return to the "loving heart" and leave printed pages aside.

Prayer is nothing more than getting into intimate contact with God. It is communication with God, and as such it need not be expressed in words, nor even articulated mentally. One can communicate with a glance of the eyes, with a smile, with a sigh, as well as by a human act. Even...the painting of a picture, or a look toward heaven or the taking of a drink of water [can be a prayer].

— Ernesto Cardenal

OUR ACTIONS CAN BE PRAYERS. Indeed, they ought to be if they come truly and spontaneously from our heart, which is also where our authentic work and actions derive from. Drinking water — if done with gratitude and awareness — is a prayer. So is painting a picture or study or dance — if it truly comes from a deep, heart place.

All our bodily acts are of the nature of prayer. Our body performs a perfect physiological act of thanksgiving when, thirsting, it receives into itself a glass of water. Or, when on a hot day we bathe in a cool river, our skin sings a hymn of thanksgiving in praise of the Creator, even though this kind of prayer may be non-rational, unconscious and at times involuntary. However we are able to transform everything we do into prayer. Work and labor are forms of existential prayer.

— Ernesto Cardenal

YES, ALL BODILY ACTS "are of the nature of prayer." Here, the dualism between body and soul, matter and spirit, loses its grip on us. Lovemaking is prayer and eating is prayer and laughter is prayer and fighting for justice is prayer and going to prison for justice is prayer. This is why I define prayer as our radical response to life. Whether awe or grief, creativity or acts of compassion, all can and ought to be our prayer.

God surrounds us on all sides like the air. And like the atmosphere he emits visible and audible waves, and we are unable to see and hear them unless we are tuning in on the proper channels. Thus the divine waves are all around us, but we are unable to identify them as coming from Him unless we are in tune with them....

All nature is charity, *but only the mystic experientially lives this kind of love. God's love surrounds us on all sides. His love is the water we drink and the air we breathe and the light we behold. All natural phenomena are but different forms of God's love. We move in His love as the fish swims in the water....His love surrounds us on all sides, but we fail to notice it, as we fail to notice the pressure of the atmosphere.*

— Ernesto Cardenal

CARDENAL SPEAKS OF OUR PANENTHEISTIC EXPERIENCE of Divinity. "God surrounds us on all sides like the air." We are in God as we are in the atmosphere, which is in fact the sky. Sky is all around us (and within us, since when we breathe, we breathe in the sky). We only see it as something blue and up there at a distance. But we are breathing it intimately every minute. We depend on it for life even though it is usually invisible. Similarly, sound waves travel through air invisibly, yet we know the source when we tune in to the proper channel.

It is the mystic's task to experience the truth that all nature is love. "All natural phenomena are but different forms of God's love." Nature and grace are wedded. Nature is grace. Nature is love. Have you had moments when you tasted this mystical understanding, known these truths? How long can you make that experience last?

Look at the birds in the sky and the lilies in the fields. Look at the sea anemone, at the humble protozoon and at the Omega Centaurus: they all do neither sow nor reap; they do not have warehouses or bank accounts or life insurance policies!

You forget that Someone at every moment takes care of every sinew of your body, controls the circulation of your blood and the functioning of all your glands. And you seem convinced that some small problem of your daily life can be solved by no one in the universe but yourself!

— Ernesto Cardenal

WE LOOK AT NATURE and find many lessons. Few creatures need warehouses, bank accounts, or life insurance to live full lives. Even our bodies work for nothing and do a pretty good job of things. With a cosmic awareness, we rediscover how interdependent we are with the whole history of the universe. We realize that beings are caring for us even in the toughest of times.

The saints were capable of seeing through the masks that cover the faces of humanity and they saw that the masks are unreal. In the innumerable faces of men they saw only one face: the face of love (that is to say, the face of Christ).

— Thomas Merton

LIKE NICOLAS OF CUSA, Merton sees the face of faces in all faces. The Cosmic Christ in all beings and all peoples. But to get to that face one must go deeper than outer appearances and the masks and roles people take on. We need to travel inside others to find the Christ there, just as we need to travel into our deepest and truest self to find the Christ in ourselves.

We conclude that the world is evil because there is so little love in it and we blame and castigate those whom we hold responsible for this lack of love. Thus a theology or ethics of punishment and retribution takes the place of the vision of love, and love becomes an idealized abstraction. The daily reality of our lives is not under the rule of love, but under the rule of law, of force and of punishment. We talk about love, but we live by hate: we hate in the name of love.... On the contrary, love is the only reality. Everything that is, is by virtue of love, and if love is not clearly evident in all things, the reason is that we ourselves have made no effort to see love in all things.

— Thomas Merton

"LOVE IS THE ONLY REALITY." Merton speaks like the mystic he is. What is your perception of "daily reality"? Is it true that our modern world seems to operate "under the rule of law, of force and of punishment," rather than "under the rule of love"? Can we take responsibility for our negative perceptions and learn to see love "clearly evident in all things"?

All things love each other. All nature is oriented toward a thou. All beings that are love are in communion with each other. All plants, all animals, all beings are fraternally united by the phenomenon of mimesis.... Thus all beings love each other or feed each other, and all are united in a gigantic process of birth and growth and reproduction and death.... All nature is in close touch and interwoven. All nature is in constant embrace. The wind which caresses me and the sun which kisses me, the air which I inhale, and the fish which swims in the water, the distant star and I who behold it: we are all in close touch with one another.

— Ernesto Cardenal

IF IT IS TRUE THAT "ALL THINGS LOVE EACH OTHER," then we are lovers among lovers. Life is not boring, nor is it a place of warfare and of survival of the fittest. It is a place of no-survival, for we all die and all beings die. The question is: Is it also a place of life-before-death and love-before-death? How much love is truly shared? And how much are we part of that love?

Though we are all in close contact, we are all incomplete. This incomplete nature of ours strives unceasingly for greater perfection, and this striving we call evolution....Man, too, is incomplete; he, too is imperfect and he, too, tends toward a Thou: *he tends toward God....All creation sighs with us, as St. Paul says, in the travails of birth, the travails of the tremendous process of evolution....All things speak to us of God, because all things sigh for God: the starry sky no less than the crickets, the immense galaxies, the striped squirrel at play all the day long, fearing everything, hiding from everything (and ever moving unconsciously toward God).*

— Ernesto Cardenal

EVOLUTION IS A STRIVING TOWARD GOD. The travail of striving and of birthing is part of the "tremendous process of evolution." All of creation "sighs with us" in this process of shaping, morphing, changing, and surviving for a while. Evolution is not an enemy of belief. It is another way of talking about belief and about being and about grasping the history of our origins and hints at our future.

We have learned a bit too late in the day that action springs not from thought but from a readiness for responsibility.... Silence in the face of evil is itself evil: God will not hold us guiltless. Not to speak is to speak. Not to act is to act.

— Dietrich Bonhoeffer

DURING WORLD WAR II, Dietrich Bonhoeffer, a Lutheran pastor and theologian, stood up against Hitler, and he was hanged for doing so. From prison he writes that action comes "from a readiness for responsibility." Like Martin Luther King Jr., he notes that good intentions, understanding, and sympathy become meaningless without expression in deed. We can write papers and books and footnotes until we die and not change anything. He reaffirms the teaching of Aquinas and others that sins of omission can be very grave because "not to speak is to speak" and "not to act is to act."

Christianity stands or falls with its revolutionary protest against violence, arbitrariness and pride of power and with its pleas for the weak. Christians are doing too little to make these points clear rather than too much. Christendom adjusts itself far too easily to the worship of power. Christians should give more offense, shock the world far more than they are doing now. Christians should take a stronger stand in favor of the weak rather than considering first the possible right of the strong.

— Dietrich Bonhoeffer

BONHOEFFER CALLS CHRISTIANS to a "revolutionary protest" against injustice and on behalf of the poor and weak. Do you agree that Christianity is far too easily involved in the worship of power? This is the way Bonhoeffer characterizes the God of the status quo, which supports the strong over the weak. Have Christians learned the lessons Bonhoeffer taught in the sixty years since he wrote these words? What contemporary instances can you name of Christians "shocking the world" in a healthy manner and for a significant cause?

In silence the conscious thinking mind comes to a stop, and the invisible presence and power are given the opportunity to function. If we really believe that the kingdom of God is within, we should be willing to leave the world until such time as we can reach, touch, and respond to the Father within.

Silence is the secret of the power of the Hawaiians. Through silence they communicated with nature. The language of silence salutes the divinity in all living things. Everything that has life has something of value to share with us, providing we are ready to experience it.

— Nana Veary

NANA VEARY TEACHES US that silence played a very great role in the spirituality of her people, the indigenous people of Hawaii. Silence was a power, a power that allowed them to communicate with nature, to listen to nature and its revelation. Silence "salutes the divinity in all living things." One Native American once said that "trees talk; they talk to each other. But the trouble with white people is they don't know how to listen." You have to be silent to hear the trees talking.

Veary calls us to let go of our "conscious thinking mind" so we can taste silence and what it has to teach us. Can you be that still?

You are made whole again in silence. Solitude shatters the illusion that you and I are separate. About eight years ago, I stopped giving classes in metaphysics and began holding silent retreats. I changed my emphasis from talking to God in prayer to listening to Him in silence. In silent retreats which last several days, you can go deeply into your consciousness. The purpose is to free yourself of anger, guilt, resentment, discouragement, disappointment, worry, all the negative thought patterns buried in the subconscious mind. In silent retreats you clear your channels so life can be fulfilled. Silent retreats give you spiritual dignity.

— Nana Veary

VEARY ENCOURAGES US to pray differently, so that prayer isn't "talking to God" but "listening to Him in silence." Silence helps us to go deep and rid ourselves of many negative patterns. In this process we find our "spiritual dignity." Do you agree? How often have you simply listened in silence to what God might have to say to you?

Silence means no repetitions, no affirmations, no denials, only a conscious acknowledgement of God's allness. In the silence, one is beyond words and thoughts. The deeper the silence, the more powerful the meditation. One's spiritual experiences in the silence are to be kept holy and sacred. The more we keep it secret and sacred, the greater the power, and there you have the mystic!

— Nana Veary

FOR NANA VEARY the very meaning of being a mystic is being at home with silence. "No repetitions, no affirmations, no denials." Power comes with the silence that takes us "beyond words and thoughts." This is not silence in the face of injustice, but silence in the face of spiritual awe. Why does Veary say to keep these latter spiritual experiences secret? Is it to turn them over in one's heart so that they teach the heart important lessons? Is it to resist any ego inflation or spiritual arrogance?

In moments of confusion such as the present, we are not left simply to our own rational contrivances. We are supported by the ultimate powers of the universe as they make themselves present to us through the spontaneities within our own beings. We need only become sensitized to these spontaneities, not with a naive simplicity, but with critical appreciation. This intimacy with our genetic endowment, and through this endowment with the larger cosmic process, is not primarily the role of the philosopher, priest, prophet or professor. It is the role of the shamanic personality, a type that is emerging once again in our society.

— Thomas Berry

GIVEN THE DEPTHS OF THE CONFUSION in our minds and institutions at this time in history, Thomas Berry counsels us that rationality will not carry the day. Rather, we should open up to and look to "the ultimate powers of the universe." How do we do this? They will reveal themselves "through the spontaneities within our own beings." Revelations come less through logic than by our being sensitive, open, and aware. This is what shamans do, and shamanism is undergoing a return in our world.

Now, in our modern scientific age, in a manner never known before, we have created our own sacred story, the epic of evolution, telling us, from empirical observation and critical analysis, how the universe came to be, the sequence of its transformations down through some billions of years, how our solar system came into being, then how the Earth took shape and brought us into existence.... This is our sacred story.

— Thomas Berry

THOMAS BERRY CELEBRATES OUR NEW, and collective, sacred story, one that permeates the globe at this time, one that is truly universal, and one that derives from science. He emphasizes in other places how important sacred stories have always been to human tribes in order to ground them in morality and in celebration. Today, the "tribe" is no longer just local. It is our entire species. Our whole species shares this common story. Do you find yourself feeling more grounded by it? Does your heart respond to it? Do you experience dance, laughter, ritual, and morality in the telling and sharing and living of it?

In relation to the earth, we have been autistic for centuries. Only now have we begun to listen with some attention and with a willingness to respond to the earth's demands that we cease our industrial assault, that we abandon our inner rage against the conditions of our earthly existence, that we renew our human participation in the grand liturgy of the universe....None of our existing cultures can deal with this situation out of its own resources. We must invent, or reinvent, a sustainable human culture by a descent into our prerational, our instinctive, resources. Our cultural resources have lost their integrity. They cannot be trusted.

— Thomas Berry

BERRY NAMES OUR INABILITY TO LISTEN to the earth as our collective "autism." We have only begun to listen to how we have harmed her. And the only way out of the dead end we find ourselves in is to listen to earth's pain and to call on our "prerational, our instinctive, resources." We must each call up the mystic in ourselves. We have to move beyond culture as we know it, civilization as we know it. What is the alternative if we do not take these steps? Where do we begin?

We will recover our sense of wonder and our sense of the sacred only if we appreciate the universe beyond ourselves as a revelatory experience of that numinous presence whence all things come into being. Indeed, the universe is the primary sacred reality. We become sacred by our participation in this more sublime dimension of the world about us.

— Thomas Berry

BERRY REMINDS US that we can recover our sense of wonder and the sacred. Thus, by implication, he says we have pretty much lost it. Do you agree? Have our sense of wonder and our sense of the sacred been diminished? Can a new relationship with the universe, with that which is the "primary sacred reality," bring this sense alive again? How might recovering our sense of wonder and the sacred lead to greater wisdom, for example, and to celebration and gratitude and even reverence for everything that is?

The evolutionary process is neither random nor determined but creative. It follows the general pattern of all creativity.... We can also understand the governing principles of evolution in terms of its three movements toward differentiation, inner spontaneity, and comprehensive bonding.

With this understanding it would be difficult to overemphasize the magnificence of this evolutionary doctrine. It provides grandeur in our view of the universe and our human role in it that is so overwhelming. Indeed, in its human expression the universe is able to reflect on itself and enjoy its grandeur in a special mode of conscious self-awareness. The evolutionary vision provides the most profound mystique of the universe.

— Thomas Berry

BERRY IS EXCITED about the grandeur and magnificence of evolution and by the "overwhelming" role that we play in the new story of the universe. He deliberately contrasts this with the mechanistic view of the universe, the deterministic view, that reduces humanity to mere chance or our being to a random collection of atoms.

He feels that when you understand creativity and the patterns it creates, you begin to understand the fuller meaning and significance not only of the universe but of our role in it. We are latecomers to the universe. But we come with a "special mode of conscious self-awareness." We can get to know the universe in a deep, personal, and even intimate way. Do you feel part of the universe in this way? Are you part of the "most profound mystique of the universe"? Are we busy creating rituals and ceremonies to tell these deep stories of belonging once again?

In our present context, failure in creativity would be an absolute failure. A present failure at this order of magnitude cannot be remedied later by a larger success. In this context a completely new type of creativity is needed. This creativity must have as its primary concern the survival of the earth in its functional integrity. Concern for the well-being of the planet is the one concern that, it is hoped, will bring the nations of the world into an international community.

— Thomas Berry

BERRY BELIEVES CREATIVITY IS THE ANSWER. Once we have listened deeply enough, we can re-create the way we live on the earth. We can create new relationships even between nations, based on the suffering of mother earth and our own needs as citizens of planet earth. But time is running out. "Failure in creativity would be an absolute failure." Are we awakening our creativity?

If Saint John and Saint Paul could think of the Christ form of the universe, if Aquinas could say that the whole universe together participates in the divine goodness more perfectly and represents it better than any single creature whatever, and if Teilhard could insist that the human gives to the entire cosmos its most sublime mode of being, then it should not be difficult to accept the universe itself as the primordial sacred community, the macrophase mode of every religious tradition, the context in which the divine reality is revealed to itself in that diversity which in a special manner is "the perfection of the universe."

— Thomas Berry

NOT ONLY CAN A DEEPENED AWARENESS of the earth and the cosmos bring nations together — it can also bring religions together, for "the universe itself [is] the primordial sacred community"; it is the context of every divine revelation. Berry sees this thread of understanding in the entire Christian tradition, from Paul and John in the New Testament to Aquinas in the Middle Ages and Teilhard de Chardin in the twentieth century. Yet the sacred cosmos inspires not just the Christian tradition but all religious traditions. It can bring us together in common work and ethics and inspiration. Are we ready?

The human venture depends absolutely on this quality of awe and reverence and joy in the Earth and all that lives and grows upon the Earth....In the end the universe can only be explained in terms of celebration. It is all an exuberant expression of existence itself....A way is opening for each person to receive the total spiritual heritage of the human community as well as the total spiritual heritage of the universe. Within this context the religious antagonisms of the past can be overcome, the particular traditions can be vitalized, and the feeling of presence to a sacred universe can appear once more to dynamize and sustain human affairs.

We must feel that we are supported by that same power that brought the Earth into being, that power that spun the galaxies into space, that tilt the sun and brought the moon into its orbit.

— Thomas Berry

BERRY CALLS FOR PROFOUND CELEBRATION as the only real explanation of, or meaning for, the universe. This idea comes very close to that of Aquinas, namely, that "sheer joy" is the cause of the universe. Do you sense a deeper joy and a more profound celebration taking over the consciousness of humans today? What can we do to make that the case? Can we find ways to spread the "exuberant expression of existence," which the universe is about and has always been about?

Berry also observes that the rivalries between religious traditions can cease in the context of the rediscovery of the universe, while at the same time we can, with a renewed awareness of the universe, revitalize our religious traditions, which are so often too self-centered. We have yearnings to feel connected to and supported by the powers that have brought the universe and its wonders into existence. Have you felt those powers? Do you help others feel them? Are these powers what we have traditionally called God or the Creator or the Goddess?

THE MYSTICAL WRITERS
IN THIS BOOK

THOMAS AQUINAS (1225–1274)

Thomas Aquinas was a genius who was recognized as such by his ambitious parents. They put him into a Benedictine monastery at the age of six in hopes that he would become abbot of Monte Casino and thus raise the family fortunes. However, at sixteen, he left the Benedictines, who like many monastic orders at that time were too comfortable and committed to a dying feudal culture. He enrolled at the University of Naples, where he encountered for the first time the upstart Dominican order and the teachings of Aristotle, newly translated by the rising influence of Muslim scholarship. He joined the Dominicans and spent the rest of his life bringing the best science of his day (which was that of Aristotle) and faith together — much to the consternation of the fundamentalists of his day, who, after he died, condemned him three times. Later he was canonized a saint.

NICOLAI BERDYAEV (1874–1948)

Nicolai Berdyaev was a Russian philosopher who stood up to the Russian aristocracy and was exiled for it; he embraced Russian Orthodox Christianity but criticized its alliance with the czar and was banished again for that. After criticizing the materialism of the Bolshevik revolution, he was banished for life from Russia. From 1922 on he spent most of his time in Paris participating in ecumenical work. He championed social justice and the role of spirit and creativity in his many writings.

Thomas Berry (1914–2009)

Thomas Berry was a priest in the Passionist order who learned Chinese and Native American languages as well as contemporary science. He called himself a "geologian" for his love of and study of the earth and its systems. Strongly influenced by Teilhard de Chardin's work, he was bent on saving the earth from a "pathological" mindset that was destroying the earth. His books include *The Dream of the Earth*, *The Great Work*, and *The Universe Story* (with Brian Swimme). He felt that the new creation story from contemporary science could assist humankind to let anthropocentrism go, and that a new (and ancient) relationship with sacred nature should form the basis of a reinvention of education, law, politics, religion, and economics.

Dietrich Bonhoeffer (1906–1945)

A Lutheran pastor who escaped the Gestapo in 1939 and went to New York City, Dietrich Bonhoeffer nevertheless voluntarily returned to Germany in order to "share the tribulations of this time with my people." He opposed Hitler and was arrested for being part of an underground movement to assassinate Hitler. He spent eighteen months in a prison (not a concentration camp) and was hanged there shortly before the Americans liberated the prison. Among his books are *Letters and Papers from Prison*, *The Cost of Discipleship*, *Creation and Fall*, and *Life Together*.

Marcus J. Borg (1942–)

Marcus Borg is a recognized New Testament scholar and retired professor of religion and culture at Oregon State University. He is currently canon theologian at Trinity Episcopal Cathedral in Portland, Oregon. His books include *Jesus: A New Vision*, *Meeting Jesus Again for the First Time*, *The Meaning of Jesus: Two Visions*, and *The Heart of Christianity*.

Ernesto Cardenal (1925–)

A Nicaraguan poet, priest, and activist, Ernesto Cardenal studied with Thomas Merton as a novice monk in Merton's Trappist community. He lived in a community in the Solentiname Islands in Nicaragua when it was bombed by the dictator Anastasio Somoza.

He was minister of culture in Nicaragua's Sandinista government and is the author of many books of poetry, including *Cosmic Canticle*.

PEDRO CASALDALIGA (1928–)

Pedro Casaldaliga is a poet and bishop in Mato Grosso in the rain forest of Brazil, where he has defended the Indians and the forest. Writer Penny Lernoux has called him "a witty, fiery, mystical, practical poet-priest, bishop of the poor, defender of the Indian, a… 'typical' priest of the church that has given the world so many saints and martyrs in just the past decade." His priests and close colleagues were arrested, tortured, and often killed by the military government that ruled Brazil. Archconservative churchmen have also attacked him, and he was silenced by the Vatican (a rare occurrence for a bishop).

M. D. CHENU (1895–1990)

A French Dominican, Father Chenu worked with the priest worker movement following World War II, and Pope Pius XII silenced him for twelve years, forbidding him to publish. A great historian and theologian, he was rehabilitated by the Second Vatican Council, where he was a primary voice behind the document on the church in the modern world. He named the creation spirituality tradition for me when I studied with him in 1968, and he was professor to Yves Congar and Edward Schillebeeckx, two prominent European Dominican theologians. He can rightly be called the grandfather of liberation theology.

BRUCE CHILTON (1949–)

An Episcopal priest, Bruce Chilton is a biblical scholar and the Bernard Iddings Bell Professor of Religion at Bard College in upstate New York. His books include *Rabbi Jesus*, *Rabbi Paul*, and *Mary Magdalene: A Biography*, as well as *The Way of Jesus: To Repair and Renew the World* and *A Galilean Rabbi and His Bible*.

JOHN DOMINIC CROSSAN (1934–)

John Dominic Crossan is professor emeritus of De Paul University and a foremost historical Jesus scholar. His books include

The Historical Jesus, Jesus: A Revolutionary Biography, The Birth of Christianity, Who Killed Jesus?, and *In Search of Paul: How Jesus's Apostle Opposed Rome's Empire with God's Kingdom* (with Jonathan L. Reed).

DOROTHY DAY (1897–1980)

Dorothy Day was an active communist in New York defending the rights of the poor when she converted to Catholicism, explaining that she needed "someone to thank" for the new life in her when she found herself pregnant. She founded the Catholic Worker movement, which offers hospitality to the poorest of the poor, and went to jail dozens of times to protest war and economic injustices.

MEISTER ECKHART (1260–1329)

Meister Eckhart was a member of the Dominican order and the most notable preacher of his time. He often preached in the German peasant dialect, and he is credited with launching the German language, since he was one of the first scholars to use German as well as Latin in his preaching. We have many of his sermons and treatises, and he can rightly be called the greatest mystic of the West. The pope condemned him a week after he died, but scholars agree it was a political condemnation since he supported women (including the Beguine movement), the peasants, and the poor in his work.

CLARISSA PINKOLA ESTÉS (1945–)

Clarissa Pinkola Estés is a senior Jungian analyst who holds a doctorate in multicultural studies and clinical psychology. She is a *cantadora*, or storyteller, as well as a scholar, poet, and philosopher whose book *Women Who Run with the Wolves* was on the *New York Times* bestseller list for 145 weeks. She draws on ancient stories, including those from her mixed Native American, Hungarian, and Latina heritage. She challenges women to become the fierce warriors they are.

WILLIAM EVERSON (1912–1994)

An early Beat poet and craftsman, William Everson was put in a camp for being a pacifist during World War II. After the war he discovered the Catholic Worker movement in Oakland, California, and converted to Catholicism. He became a Dominican brother and was known as Brother Antoninus while he conducted many poetry readings on university campuses around the country. He eventually left the Dominicans and taught at the University of California at Santa Cruz. Meanwhile, he continued to write poetry and essays and operate his beloved printing press, living in the woods near Santa Cruz. Strongly influenced by Robinson Jeffers, he has been called "the most important religious poet of the last half of the twentieth century."

FRANCIS OF ASSISI (1182–1226)

Francis of Assisi founded the Franciscan order in response to the growing need for reform in the church in the early thirteenth century. Opposing the comfort and security of the monastic establishment, he was also highly suspicious of the new capitalism that was emerging to replace the era's feudalism. He followed a path of voluntary poverty, simplicity, and kinship with animals, plants, and nature — advocating a way to find Christ among the poor and those without a voice.

BEDE GRIFFITHS (1906–1993)

An English Benedictine monk, Bede Griffiths chose to be a missionary in India, where he lived for over fifty years. The ashram where he stayed, Shantivanam, blended Christian and Hindu ways. He wrote many books, including *The Golden String*, *Return to the Center*, *The Marriage of East and West*, and *The Cosmic Revelation*.

HILDEGARD OF BINGEN (1098–1179)

Hildegard of Bingen was a Benedictine abbess originally in a Celtic monastery on the Rhine River in Germany. She was a gifted musician, poet, painter, scientist, and healer whose ten books cover subjects from medicine to rocks to theology and visionary sayings. One can rightly call her a "renaissance woman," and she preached and wrote letters to church hierarchy that were often critical of the priests and establishment of her day.

JESUS OF NAZARETH (c. 4 BC– c. AD 34)

Jesus of Nazareth, or the historical Jesus, launched an amazing spiritual revolution from his roots as a Jewish peasant, one who drew on the wisdom tradition and the prophetic tradition of his ancestors. A savvy and courageous social revolutionary, he preached and practiced a message of radical egalitarianism while challenging the sacrosanct social rules of his day around class, gender, and status. He taught principally through parables and aphorisms; both are ways of teaching that require participation and thinking on behalf of listeners. He was crucified by the Roman Empire for his claims that compassion and justice trump imperial rule.

The canonical Jesus is the person called Christ, or the "risen Christ," who speaks after the death of Jesus (the Buddhists call the post-death Buddha the "living Buddha"). Christ's words were not spoken by the historical Jesus; they were words put into his mouth by Jesus' community of followers. These people were so taken by his message — and by the story of Jesus' life, death, and resurrection, including the sending of the Spirit — that they were moved to "fill in" the teachings from Jesus with more images and words of wisdom.

JOHN OF THE CROSS (1542–1591)

John of the Cross was a Spanish Carmelite who shortly after being ordained a priest was enlisted by Teresa of Avila to join her project of reforming the Carmelite order. Teresa was working on the women, and she wanted John to work on the men. He was kidnapped and imprisoned twice (having escaped the first imprisonment) and had been tortured almost to death when he eventually escaped the second imprisonment. While in prison and afterward, he wrote poetry about the search for God, the lost Beloved, the dark night, and other movements of the soul's deep journeys.

JULIAN OF NORWICH (1342–c. 1416)

Julian of Norwich has been called the first woman of English letters. She was a hermitess who chose to live in a sealed-up apartment adjacent to a church sanctuary. Even though she lived through the Black Death, her book *Revelations of Divine Love* is a profound and beautiful and hopeful book about the soul's work, yet it was not published until the seventeenth century.

MARTIN LUTHER KING JR. (1929–1968)

A son of a Baptist minister in Atlanta, Georgia, Martin Luther King Jr. led the civil rights movement of the late fifties and sixties. Best known perhaps for his "I Have a Dream" speech at the March on Washington to demand civil rights legislation, he was imprisoned thirty-nine times and died a martyr at the age of thirty-nine to the cause of racial justice and harmony. He took a public stand against the Vietnam War shortly before he was assassinated.

MECHTILD OF MAGDEBURG (1210–C. 1282)

Mechtild of Magdeburg was a German laywoman who was a member of the Beguine movement, which comprised laywomen who were not married and were not nuns. They lived in communities and often worked with the poor, the young, and the sick. They regularly made their living as artisans. She kept a journal all her life, which was later published and entitled *Flowing Light of the Godhead.* The movement was attacked by the pope, who condemned the women seventeen times, and by many threatened clergy.

THOMAS MERTON (1915–1968)

Thomas Merton was a contemplative monk in the Trappist order at Gethsemani Abbey in Kentucky. His prolific writings covered not just the inner life but cultural issues and East/West spiritual encounters. He came out against the Vietnam War even before Martin Luther King Jr. did. Merton died a mysterious death (some say he was murdered) while in Bangkok, Thailand, after giving a lecture to a group of nuns and monks on Karl Marx and monasticism. During his final pilgrimage to the East, he had a profound spiritual experience at a Buddhist shrine, and on that journey he wrote frequently in his notebook, "Eckhart is my lifeboat."

NICOLAS OF CUSA (1400–1464)

A significant scientist and mathematician, Nicolas of Cusa lived at the cusp of the sixteenth-century Renaissance. A cardinal in the Roman Catholic Church, he was assigned to Greece, where he was in a minority. He wrote some very progressive observations about deep ecumenism and the wisdom common to all religions. The late physicist David Bohm said he owed more to Cusa than to Einstein.

PAUL OF TARSUS (died c. AD 64)

The biblical writer Paul was a Jewish zealot who at first persecuted the followers of Jesus but then had a conversion experience that rendered him a powerful follower and teacher of Jesus' message of a kingdom of God in which justice and equality ruled, as distinct from the dominant power of the Roman Empire. Like Jesus, he paid the ultimate price for this teaching, being killed by the Romans in Rome. Paul was the first writer in the Christian Bible, writing seven New Testament letters years before the Gospels were put together, and he was the first Christian theologian. His special outreach was to the gentiles.

OSCAR ROMERO (1917–1980)

Oscar Romero was archbishop of El Salvador at the start of the civil war that ravaged that country from the late 1970s through the 1980s. Though initially siding with conservative landowners who controlled the land and wealth, he came to see the ravages the unjust system wreaked on ordinary people. He subsequently spoke out on behalf of social justice and against the military that was carrying out much violence against the poor. For his efforts he was constantly harassed by the Vatican, and eventually he was murdered and martyred by the military, killed while celebrating Mass.

E. F. SCHUMACHER (1911–1977)

A Rhodes Scholar in economics, an economic adviser in postwar Germany, and the top economist and head of planning at the British Coal Board, E. F. Schumacher shocked the world with his "heretical" teaching — presented in his classic book *Small Is Beautiful: Economics as if People Mattered* — that denied that bigger is better and more is superior. He critiqued the simplification of quantification that underscores so much economics and called instead for quality-of-life indicators such as health, beauty, and permanence. He studied Buddhism in depth and converted to Catholicism later in his life.

DOROTHEE SOELLE (1929–2003)

Dorothee Soelle was a leading feminist liberation theologian, poet, activist, and author of many books, including *Political Theology*, *Suffering*, *Theology for Skeptics*, and *Revolutionary Patience*. Born in Germany, she taught for twelve years at Union Theological Seminary in New York City. She emphasized the role that mysticism, such as that of Meister Eckhart, can play in the struggle for social and gender justice.

TEILHARD DE CHARDIN (1881–1955)

Pierre Teilhard de Chardin was a scientist, poet, mystic, and Jesuit priest who spent his life trying to bring science and religion together. When the Jesuit order banished him to China, he worked on the Peking Man expeditions in that country and published many scientific articles. He was forbidden to publish most of his philosophical writings during his lifetime, but he left them in the hands of a woman friend who saw that they were published after he died. Spirit and matter joining was his main interest, and incarnation and the Cosmic Christ were important theological categories.

TERESA OF AVILA (1515–1582)

A sixteenth-century Carmelite nun in Spain, Teresa of Avila attempted a reformation of her order and managed to dance out of the hands of the Inquisition while writing four books and founding seventeen convents. These strict convents adhered to the original values of her order, and they were needed because much of her order had fallen into laxity. She was canonized a saint forty years after her death and declared a doctor of the church in 1970.

HOWARD THURMAN (1899–1981)

A grandson of slaves, Howard Thurman grew up in Florida close to the earth and to the ocean. Though very poor, he managed to attend college. He and his wife visited Gandhi in the thirties, and he brought Gandhi's teachings of nonviolence back to the United States. He deeply influenced Dr. Martin Luther King Jr., who took Thurman's book *Jesus and the Disinherited* with him each of the thirty-nine times he went to jail. The last decades of Thurman's life were spent as pastor at the Church of the Fellowship of All Peoples in San Francisco, which was consciously interfaith and interracial. His books and sermons are profound and poetically inspired.

Nana Veary (1908–1993)

Nana Veary was an indigenous Hawaiian and a spiritual teacher whose religious journey began in Christian Pentecostalism and led her to Buddhism, Science of the Mind, and beyond. She tells her story in her book, *Change We Must: My Spiritual Journey*, which brims with the wisdom of an elder. She writes: "There is an interior Christ-Mind that baffles all reasoning and is beyond all human explanation."

ACKNOWLEDGMENTS

I wish to thank Jason Gardner, my editor at New World Library, and also Jeff Campbell and Kristen Cashman for their editing and improvements. I wish to thank all of the mystics, living and deceased, cited in this book, who have gifted me and so many others with their wisdom and their sharing. A special note of appreciation to Dr. Clarissa Pinkola Estés, for her guidance and encouragement and generous editing of her work. I also wish to thank my many students over a period of forty years of teaching in many colleges and on several continents. They have posed the questions and aroused the enthusiasm and shared the stories that continue to convince me of the power of the mystics both to heal and to challenge. May our common adventure never slow down!

ENDNOTES

Day 1: Luke 17:21.

Day 2: Luke 17:21. Translation by the author.

Day 3: Bruce Chilton, *Rabbi Jesus: An Intimate Biography* (New York: Doubleday, 2000), 18–19.

Day 4: Ibid., 19.

Day 5: Ibid., 54.

Day 6: John 9:5.

Day 7: Matthew Fox, *Meditations with Meister Eckhart* (Santa Fe, NM: Bear & Co, 1983), 33.

Day 8: Sue Woodruff, *Meditations with Mechtild of Magdeburg* (Santa Fe, NM: Bear & Co., 1982), 58.

Day 9: Ibid., 34.

Day 10: Fox, *Meditations with Meister Eckhart*, 12.

Day 11: *Gospel of Thomas*, Saying 77. Translation in Robert W. Funk, Roy W. Hoover, and the Jesus Seminar, *The Five Gospels: What Did Jesus Really Say?* (San Francisco: HarperSanFrancisco, 1997), 515.

Day 12: Chilton, *Rabbi Jesus*, 73–74.

Day 13: 1 John 4:16.

Day 14: Matthew 25:31–40, 25:45.

Day 15: Marcus J. Borg, *Meeting Jesus Again for the First Time* (San Francisco: HarperSanFrancisco, 1994), 75, 81, 88.

Day 16: John Dominic Crossan, *The Essential Jesus: Original Sayings and Earliest Images* (San Francisco: HarperSanFrancisco, 1994), 3.

Day 17: Ibid., 12, 23.

Day 18: John Dominic Crossan, *Jesus: A Revolutionary Biography* (San Francisco: HarperSanFrancisco, 1994), 181.

Day 19: Fox, *Meditations with Meister Eckhart*, 49.

Day 20: Gabriele Uhlein, *Meditations with Hildegard of Bingen* (Santa Fe, NM: Bear & Co., 1982), 58.

Day 21: Ibid., 51.

Day 22: Ibid.

Day 23: Ibid., 41.

Day 24: Matthew Fox, *Passion for Creation: The Earth-Honoring Spirituality of Meister Eckhart* (Rochester, VT: Inner Traditions, 2000), 198.

Day 25: Uhlein, *Meditations with Hildegard of Bingen*, 30.

Day 26: Ibid., 28.

Day 27: Ibid., 24.

Day 28: Galatians 2:20, 2 Corinthians 3:18.

Day 29: Bruce Chilton, *Rabbi Paul: An Intellectual Biography* (New York: Doubleday, 2004), 248–49, 207. John Dominic Crossan and Jonathan L. Reed, *In Search of Paul* (San Francisco: HarperSanFrancisco, 2004), 278, 283.

Day 30: Uhlein, *Meditations with Hildegard of Bingen*, 21, 90.

Day 31: Eloi Leclerc, trans., *The Canticle of Creatures: Symbols of Union* (Chicago: Franciscan Herald Press, 1970), xvii–xviii.

Day 32: M. D. Chenu, *Nature, Man, and Society in the Twelfth Century* (Chicago: University of Chicago Press, 1968), 239.

Day 33: Ibid., 269.

Day 34: Brendan Doyle, *Meditations with Julian of Norwich* (Santa Fe, NM: Bear & Co., 1983), 32.

Day 35: Ibid., 29.

Day 36: Ibid., 25.

Day 37: Ibid., 123.

Day 38: Ibid., 119, 113.

Day 39: Ibid., 114.

Day 40: Ibid., 106, 108.

Day 41: Ibid., 104.

Day 42: Ibid., 103, 90.

Day 43: Ibid., 97, 92.

Day 44: Ibid., 95.

Day 45: Ibid., 69, 74, 88.

Day 46: Ibid., 89.

Day 47: Ibid., 85.

Day 48: Ibid., 82.

Day 49: Ibid., 78.

Day 50: Ibid., 77.

Day 51: Ibid., 69.

Day 52: Fox, *Meditations with Meister Eckhart*, 34.

Day 53: Doyle, *Meditations with Julian of Norwich*, 67.

Day 54: Ibid., 62.

Day 55: Ibid., 60.

Day 56: Ibid., 61.

Day 57: Ibid., 58, 53.

Day 58: Ibid., 47.

Day 59: Ibid., 44.

Day 60: Ibid., 42.

Day 61: Woodruff, *Meditations with Mechtild of Magdeburg*, 69.

Day 62: Ibid., 60–61.

Day 63: Ibid., 62.

Day 64: Ibid., 47.

Day 65: Ibid., 46.

Day 66: Ibid., 42.

Day 67: Ibid., 39.

Day 68: Ibid., 38.

Day 69: Ibid., 36.

Day 70: Ibid., 37.

Day 71: Ibid., 34.

Day 72: Ibid., 35.

Day 73: Ibid., 31.

Day 74: Ibid., 26.

Day 75: Matthew Fox, *Sheer Joy: Conversations with Thomas Aquinas on Creation Spirituality* (New York: Jeremy Tarcher/Putnam, 2003), 120.

Day 76: Ibid.

Day 77: Ibid., 121.

Day 78: Ibid., 119.

Day 79: Ibid., 118.

Day 80: Ibid., 113.

Day 81: Ibid., 112.

Day 82: Ibid., 113.

Day 83: Ibid., 112–13.

Day 84: Ibid.

Day 85: Ibid., 228.

Day 86: Ibid., 231.

Day 87: Ibid., 233.

Day 88: Ibid., 111.

Day 89: Ibid., 109–10.

Day 90: Ibid., 109.

Day 91: Ibid., 104.

Day 92: Ibid.

Day 93: Ibid., 102.

Day 94: Ibid., 101.

Day 95: Ibid., 100.

Day 96: Ibid., 99.

Day 97: Ibid., 98.

Day 98: Ibid., 78–79.

Day 99: Ibid., 76.

Day 100: Ibid., 75.

Day 101: Ibid., 72, 71.

Day 102: Ibid, 69.

Day 103: Ibid., 66.

Day 104: Ibid., 65.

Day 105: Ibid., 248.

Day 106: Ibid., 251.

Day 107: Ibid., 64.

Day 108: Ibid., 60.

Day 109: Ibid.

Day 110: Chenu, *Nature, Man, and Society*, 238.

Day 111: Fox, *Sheer Joy*, 234.

Day 112: Ibid., 210.

Day 113: Ibid., 210–11.

Day 114: Ibid., 278.

Day 115: Ibid., 279.

Day 116: Ibid., 261.

Day 117: Ibid., 256.

Day 118: Ibid., 260.

Day 119: Ibid., 298.

Day 120: Ibid., 306.

Day 121: Ibid., 326.

Day 122: Ibid., 329.

Day 123: Ibid., 333.

Day 124: Ibid., 338.

Day 125: Ibid., 343, 340, 346.

Day 126: Ibid., 350–51.

Day 127: Ibid., 383.

Day 128: Fox, *Meditations with Meister Eckhart*, 64.

Day 129: Fox, *Passion for Creation*, 217.

Day 130: Fox, *Meditations with Meister Eckhart*, 51.

Day 131: Ibid., 46.

Day 132: Ibid., 45.

Day 133: Ibid.

Day 134: Ibid., 44.

Day 135: Fox, *Passion for Creation*, 76.

Day 136: Ibid., 76–77.

Day 137: Ibid., 381, 384.

Day 138: Ibid., 214, 215, 217.

Day 139: Ibid., 464.

Day 140: Ibid.

Day 141: Ibid., 119.

Day 142: Ibid., 112.

Day 143: Ibid., 116.

Day 144: Ibid., 99.

Day 145: Ibid., 98.

Day 146: Fox, *Meditations with Meister Eckhart*, 96, 108.

Day 147: Ibid., 90.

Day 148: Ibid., 81, 74.

Day 149: Bruce Chilton, *The Way of Jesus: To Repair and Renew the World* (Nashville: Abingdon Press, 2010), 139.

Day 150: James Francis Yockey, *Meditations with Nicholas of Cusa* (Santa Fe, NM: Bear & Co., 1987), 139.

Day 151: Ibid., 140.

Day 152: Ibid., 133, 132.

Day 153: Ibid., 138.

Day 154: Ibid., 126.

Day 155: Ibid., 29.

Day 156: Ibid., 123.

Day 157: Ibid., 118–19.

Day 158: Ibid., 112–13.

Day 159: Ibid., 110–11.

Day 160: Ibid., 107.

Day 161: Ibid., 87–88.

Day 162: Ibid., 69.

Day 163: Ibid., 64, 67.

Day 164: Ibid., 62–63.

Day 165: Ibid., 60.

Day 166: Ibid., 52.

Day 167: Ibid., 49, 46.

Day 168: Ibid., 33.

Day 169: Ibid., 32.

Day 170: Kieran Kavanaugh and Otilio Rodriguez, trans., *The Collected Works of St. John of the Cross* (Washington, DC: ICS Publications, 1973), 412.

Day 171: E. Allison Peers, trans., *Interior Castle by St. Teresa of Avila* (New York: Doubleday Image, 1961), 234.

Day 172: E. F. Schumacher, *Small Is Beautiful: Economics as if People Mattered* (New York: Harper & Row, 1973), 31.

Day 173: Ibid., 156–57.

Day 174: Ibid., 79–80, 82.

Day 175: Teofilo Cabestrero, *Mystic of Liberation: A Portrait of Bishop Pedro Casaldaliga of Brazil* (Maryknoll, NY: Orbis Books, 1981), 164.

Day 176: Ibid.

Day 177: Ibid., 166.

Day 178: Steven Herrmann, *William Everson: The Shaman's Call: Interviews, Introduction and Commentaries* (New York: Eloquent Books, 2009), 87.

Day 179: Ibid.

Day 180: Ibid., 87, 35–36.

Day 181: Ibid., 41, notes 62, 63.

Day 182: Ibid., 266.

Day 183: Ibid., 265.

Day 184: Ibid., 265–66; William Everson, *Naked Heart: Talking on Poetry, Mysticism & the Erotic* (Albuquerque, NM: An American Poetry Book, 1992), 172.

Day 185: Herrmann, *William Everson: The Shaman's Call*, 264–65.

Day 186: Ibid., 137.

Day 187: Ibid., 141.

Day 188: William Everson, *River-Root: A Syzygy* (Seattle: Broken Moon Press, 1990), 17.

Day 189: Ibid.

Day 190: Ibid., 17–18.

Day 191: Ibid., 18.

Day 192: Ibid., 24.

Day 193: Ibid., 26, 27.

Day 194: Lee Bartlett, ed., *Earth Poetry: Selected Essays & Interviews of William Everson 1950/1977* (Berkeley: Oyez, 1980), 17.

Day 195: Ibid., 18–19.

Day 196: Everson, *Naked Heart*, 136–37.

Day 197: Ibid., 129.

Day 198: Ibid., 252.

Day 199: Ibid.

Day 200: Ibid., 253.

Day 201: Ibid., 253–54.

Day 202: Ibid., 254.

Day 203: Howard Thurman, *The Search for Common Ground* (Richmond, IN: Friends United Press, 1986), 8.

Day 204: Howard Thurman, *Jesus and the Disinherited* (Richmond, IN: Friends United Press, 1981), 112.

Day 205: Ibid., 108.

Day 206: Ibid., 108–9.

Day 207: Ibid., 108.

Day 208: Ibid., 49.

Day 209: Ibid., 50.

Day 210: Howard Thurman, *The Luminous Darkness* (Richmond, IN: Friends United Press, 1989), 94.

Day 211: Howard Thurman, *The Creative Encounter* (Richmond, IN: Friends United Press, 1972), 123–24.

Day 212: Howard Thurman, *Deep Is the Hunger* (Richmond, IN: Friends United Press, 1973), 108–9.

Day 213: Thurman, *Jesus and the Disinherited*, 28–29.

Day 214: Thurman, *The Creative Encounter*, 152.

Day 215: Howard Thurman, *Disciplines of the Spirit* (Richmond, IN: Friends United Press, 1977), 14.

Day 216: Thurman, *The Search for Common Ground*, 83.

Day 217: Ibid., 83–84.

Day 218: Teilhard de Chardin, *Writings in Time of War* (New York: Harper & Row, 1968), 262.

Day 219: Letter written in 1920, cited in Robert Speaight, *The Life of Teilhard de Chardin* (New York: Harper & Row, 1967), 109.

Day 220: Teilhard de Chardin, *The Heart of Matter* (New York: Harcourt Brace Jovanovich, 1978), 71.

Day 221: Ibid., 36, 32.

Day 222: Ibid., 26–27.

Day 223: Ibid., 28.

Day 224: Teilhard de Chardin, *Human Energy* (New York Harcourt Brace Jovanovich, 1978), 82.

Day 225: Teilhard de Chardin, *Hymn of the Universe* (New York: Harper & Row, 1965), 22.

Day 226: Teilhard, *Heart of Matter*, 25.

Day 227: Ibid., 71.

Day 228: Teilhard, *Human Energy*, 72; Teilhard de Chardin, *Letters to Two Friends* (New York: New American Library, 1968), 182.

Day 229: Teilhard, *Human Energy*, 74.

Day 230: Ibid.

Day 231: Teilhard de Chardin, *The Divine Milieu* (New York: Harper & Row, 1960), 66.

Day 232: Teilhard, *Human Energy*, 37.

Day 233: Teilhard de Chardin, *Christianity and Evolution* (New York: Harcourt Brace Jovanovich, 1971), 92.

Day 234: Speaight, *The Life of Teilhard de Chardin*, 156.

Day 235: Teilhard, *Hymn of the Universe*, 23.

Day 236: Bede Griffiths, *The Marriage of East and West* (Tucson, AZ: Medio Media, 2003), 186.

Day 237: Ibid., 186.

Day 238: Ibid., 179–80.

Day 239: Ibid., 153.

Day 240: Ibid., 202.

Day 241: Ibid., 157.

Day 242: Ibid.

Day 243: Ibid., 158.

Day 244: Ibid., 151–52.

Day 245: Ibid., 199.

Day 246: Ibid.

Day 247: Ibid., 200.

Day 248: Bede Griffiths, *Christ in India: Essays towards a Hindu-Christian Dialogue* (Springfield, IL: Templegate Publishers, 1984), 127–28.

Day 249: Ibid., 129.

Day 250: Ibid., 20.

Day 251: Ibid., 20–21.

Day 252: Bede Griffiths, *Cosmic Revelation: The Hindu Way to God* (Springfield, IL: Templegate Publishers, 1983), 21, 22–23.

Day 253: Ibid., 44.

Day 254: Bede Griffiths, *Return to the Center* (Springfield, IL: Templegate Publishers, 1977), 105.

Day 255: Ibid., 105–6.

Day 256: Ibid., 103.

Day 257: Ibid., 98–99.

Day 258: Ibid., 86–87.

Day 259: Ibid., 78.

Day 260: Ibid., 76.

Day 261: Ibid., 35–36.

Day 262: Nicolas Berdyaev, "Salvation and Creativity: Two Understandings of Christianity," in Matthew Fox, ed., *Western Spirituality: Historical Roots, Ecumenical Routes* (Santa Fe, NM: Bear & Co., 1981), 123–24, 129.

Day 263: Nicolas Berdyaev, *The Divine and the Human* (London: Geoffrey Bles, 1949), 183.

Day 264: Ibid., 201–2.

Day 265: http://luterano.blogspot.com/2006/07/top-10-romero-quotes.html; http://onlineministries.creighton.edu/CollaborativeMinistry/romero.html.

Day 266: Dorothee Soelle, *Revolutionary Patience*, trans. Rita and Robert Kimber (Maryknoll, NY: Orbis Books, 1977), 40–41.

Day 267: Ibid., 40.

Day 268: Ibid., 42–43.

Day 269: Ibid., 22.

Day 270: Ibid.

Day 271: Ibid., 23.

Day 272: Ibid.

Day 273: Ibid., 7.

Day 274: Dorothee Soelle, *Theology for Skeptics: Reflections on God* (Minneapolis: Fortress Press, 1995), 92.

Day 275: Ibid.

Day 276: Ibid., 93.

Day 277: Ibid., 49–50.

Day 278: Ibid., 50.

Day 279: Ibid., 43–44.

Day 280: Ibid., 43.

Day 281: Clarissa Pinkola Estés, *Women Who Run with the Wolves* (New York: Ballantine Books, 1992), 6.

Day 282: Ibid.

Day 283: Ibid., 7.

Day 284: Ibid.

Day 285: Ibid., 8.

Day 286: Ibid., 9–10.

Day 287: Ibid., 10–11.

Day 288: Ibid., 11.

Day 289: Ibid., 12–13.

Day 290: Ibid., 435–36.

Day 291: Ibid., 149.

Day 292: Ibid.

Day 293: Ibid., 75.

Day 294: Ibid., 316.

Day 295: Ibid., 317.

Day 296: Ibid.

Day 297: Ibid., 213.

Day 298: Ibid., 129.

Day 299: Ibid., 335–36.

Day 300: Thomas Merton, *Contemplation in a World of Action* (Garden City, NY: Doubleday Image, 1973), 343–44.

Day 301: Ibid., 358.

Day 302: Dorothy Day, *Meditations* (New York: Newman Press, 1970), 8.

Day 303: Ibid.

Day 304: Ibid., 79–80, 37.

Day 305: Merton, *Contemplation in a World of Action*, 358–59.

Day 306: Thomas Merton, *Conjectures of a Guilty Bystander* (Garden City, NY: Doubleday Image, 1968), 296.

Day 307: Ibid., 297.

Day 308: Ibid., 301.

Day 309: Ibid., 304.

Day 310: Ibid., 307.

Day 311: Sister Therese Lentfoehr, *Words and Silence: On the Poetry of Thomas Merton* (New York: New Directions, 1979), 54.

Day 312: Ibid., 58.

Day 313: Ibid., 55–56.

Day 314: Thomas Merton, *Contemplative Prayer* (Garden City, NY: Doubleday Image, 1971), 113.

Day 315: Ibid., 70.

Day 316: Ibid., 84.

Day 317: Ibid., 85.

Day 318: Ibid., 90.

Day 319: Thomas Merton, *New Seeds of Contemplation* (New York: New Directions, 1961), 186–87.

Day 320: Ibid., 187.

Day 321: Ibid., 1.

Day 322: Thomas Merton, *The New Man* (New York: Farrar, Strauss & Giroux, 1978), 160–61.

Day 323: Ibid., 165.

Day 324: Martin Luther King Jr., *Why We Can't Wait* (New York: New American Library, 1963), 90.

Day 325: Ibid., 90.

Day 326: Ibid.., 91–92.

Day 327: Ibid., 92.

Day 328: Ibid., 92.

Day 329: M. D. Chenu, *Faith and Theology* (New York: Macmillan, 1968), 135–36.

Day 330: Ibid., 136.

Day 331: Ibid., 174.

Day 332: Ibid., 114, 113.

Day 333: Ibid., 115.

Day 334: Ernesto Cardenal, *To Live Is to Love: Meditations on Love and Spirituality* (Garden City, NY: Doubleday Image, 1974), 88.

Day 335: Ibid.

Day 336: Ibid.

Day 337: Ibid., 89.

Day 338: Ibid.

Day 339: Ibid., 92.

Day 340: Ibid., 80–81.

Day 341: Ibid., 81.

Day 342: Ibid.

Day 343: Ibid., 83.

Day 344: Ibid., 34.

Day 345: Ibid.

Day 346: Ibid.

Day 347: Ibid., 35, 52.

Day 348: Ibid., 52–53.

Day 349: Ibid., 9. Ernesto Cardenal was a pupil of Thomas Merton in the novitiate of the Abbey of Gethsemani before he returned to his homeland in Nicaragua.

Day 350: Ibid., 7.

Day 351: Ibid., 23.

Day 352: Ibid., 24–25.

Day 353: Dietrich Bonhoeffer, *Letters and Papers from Prison* (New York: Touchstone, 1997), 298.

Day 354: Dietrich Bonhoeffer, *Sermon on II Cor: 12:9*, in *Dietrich Bonhoeffer Works, Volume 13: London, 1933–1935* (Minneapolis: Augsburg Fortress, 2007), 402.

Day 355: Nana Veary, *Change We Must: My Spiritual Journey* (Honolulu, HI: Institute of Zen Studies, 1989), 104.

Day 356: Ibid., 101.

Day 357: Ibid., 103–4.

Day 358: Thomas Berry, *The Dream of the Earth* (San Francisco: Sierra Club Books, 1988), 211.

Day 359: Thomas Berry, *The Great Work: Our Way into the Future* (New York: Bell Tower, 1999), 31

Day 360: Berry, *Dream of the Earth*, 215, 207–8.

Day 361: Berry, *The Great Work*, 49

Day 362: Ibid., 169–70.

Day 363: Berry, *Dream of the Earth*, 218–19.

Day 364: Anne Lonergan and Caroline Richards, *Thomas Berry and the New Cosmology* (Mystic, CT: Twenty-Third Publications, 1987), 38.

Day 365: Berry, *The Great Work*, 166, 170, 174

BIBLIOGRAPHY

The citations in this book are taken from the following texts.

Bartlett, Lee, ed. *Earth Poetry: Selected Essays & Interviews of William Everson 1950/1977*. Berkeley: Oyez, 1980.

Berdyaev, Nicolas. *The Divine and the Human*. London: Geoffrey Bles, 1949.

Berry, Thomas. *The Dream of the Earth*. San Francisco: Sierra Club Books, 1988.

———. *The Great Work: Our Way into the Future*. New York: Bell Tower, 1999.

Bonhoeffer, Dietrich. *Letters and Papers from Prison*. New York: Touchstone: 1997.

———. *Sermon on II Cor: 12:9*. In *Dietrich Bonhoeffer Works*, Volume 13: *London, 1933–1935*. Minneapolis: Augsburg Fortress, 2007.

Borg, Marcus J. *Meeting Jesus Again for the First Time*. San Francisco: HarperSanFrancisco, 1994.

Cabestrero, Teofilo. *Mystic of Liberation: A Portrait of Bishop Pedro Casaldaliga of Brazil*. Maryknoll, NY: Orbis Books, 1981.

Cardenal, Ernesto. *To Live Is to Love: Meditations on Love and Spirituality*. Garden City, NY: Doubleday Image, 1974.

Chenu, M. D. *Faith and Theology*. New York: Macmillan, 1968.

———. *Nature, Man, and Society in the Twelfth Century*. Chicago: University of Chicago Press, 1968.

Chilton, Bruce. *Rabbi Jesus: An Intimate Biography*. New York: Doubleday, 2000.

———. *Rabbi Paul: An Intellectual Biography*. New York: Doubleday, 2004.

———. *The Way of Jesus: To Repair and Renew the World*. Nashville: Abingdon Press, 2010.

Crossan, John Dominic. *The Essential Jesus: Original Sayings and Earliest Images*. San Francisco: HarperSanFrancisco, 1994.

———. *Jesus: A Revolutionary Biography*. San Francisco: HarperSanFrancisco, 1994.

Crossan, John Dominic, and Jonathan L. Reed. *In Search of Paul*. San Francisco: HarperSanFrancisco, 2004.

Day, Dorothy. *Meditations*. New York: Newman Press, 1970.

Doyle, Brendan. *Meditations with Julian of Norwich*. Santa Fe, NM: Bear & Co., 1983.

Estés, Clarissa Pinkola. *Women Who Run with the Wolves*. New York: Ballantine Books, 1992.

Everson, William. *Naked Heart: Talking on Poetry, Mysticism & the Erotic*. Albuquerque, NM: An American Poetry Book, 1992.

————. *River-Root: A Syzygy*. Seattle: Broken Moon Press, 1990.

Fox, Matthew. *Illuminations of Hildegard of Bingen*. Santa Fe, NM: Bear & Co., 1985.

————. *Meditations with Meister Eckhart*. Santa Fe, NM: Bear & Co, 1983.

————. *Passion for Creation: The Earth-Honoring Spirituality of Meister Eckhart*. Rochester, VT: Inner Traditions, 2000.

————. *Sheer Joy: Conversations with Thomas Aquinas on Creation Spirituality*. New York: Jeremy Tarcher/Putnam, 2003.

————. ed. *Western Spirituality: Historical Roots, Ecumenical Routes*. Santa Fe, NM: Bear & Co., 1981.

Funk, Robert W., Roy W. Hoover, and the Jesus Seminar. *The Five Gospels: What Did Jesus Really Say?* San Francisco: HarperSanFrancisco, 1997.

Griffiths, Bede. *Christ in India: Essays towards a Hindu-Christian Dialogue*. Springfield, IL: Templegate Publishers, 1984.

————. *Cosmic Revelation: The Hindu Way to God*. Springfield, IL: Templegate Publishers, 1983.

————. *The Marriage of East and West*. Tucson, AZ: Medio Media, 2003.

————. *Return to the Center*. Springfield, IL: Templegate Publishers, 1977.

Herrmann, Steven. *William Everson: The Shaman's Call: Interviews, Introduction and Commentaries*. New York: Eloquent Books, 2009.

Kavanaugh, Kieran, and Otilio Rodriguez, trans. *The Collected Works of St. John of the Cross*. Washington, DC: ICS Publications, 1973.

King, Martin Luther, Jr. *Why We Can't Wait*. New York: New American Library, 1963.

Leclerc, Eloi, trans. *The Canticle of Creatures: Symbols of Union*. Chicago: Franciscan Herald Press, 1970.

Lentfoehr, Sister Therese. *Words and Silence: On the Poetry of Thomas Merton*. New York: New Directions, 1979.

Lonergan, Anne, and Caroline Richards. *Thomas Berry and the New Cosmology*. Mystic, CT: Twenty-Third Publications, 1987.

Merton, Thomas. *Conjectures of a Guilty Bystander*. Garden City, NY: Doubleday Image, 1968.

————. *Contemplation in a World of Action*. Garden City, NY: Doubleday Image, 1973.

————. *Contemplative Prayer*. Garden City, NY: Doubleday Image, 1971.

————. *The New Man*. New York: Farrar, Strauss & Giroux, 1978.

————. *New Seeds of Contemplation*. New York: New Directions, 1961.

Peers, E. Allison, trans. *Interior Castle by St. Teresa of Avila*. New York: Doubleday Image, 1961.

Schumacher, E. F. *Small Is Beautiful: Economics as if People Mattered*. New York: Harper & Row, 1973.

Soelle, Dorothee. *Revolutionary Patience*. Translated by Rita and Robert Kimber. Maryknoll, NY: Orbis Books, 1977.

————. *Theology for Skeptics: Reflections on God*. Minneapolis: Fortress Press, 1995.

Speaight, Robert. *The Life of Teilhard de Chardin*. New York: Harper & Row, 1967.

Teilhard de, Chardin. *Christianity and Evolution*. New York: Harcourt Brace Jovanovich, 1971.

————. *The Divine Milieu*. New York: Harper & Row, 1960.

————. *The Heart of Matter*. New York: Harcourt Brace Jovanovich, 1978.

————. *Human Energy*. New York: Harcourt Brace Jovanovich, 1978.

————. *Hymn of the Universe*. New York: Harper & Row, 1965.

————. *Letters to Two Friends*. New York: New American Library, 1968.

————. *Writings in Time of War*. New York: Harper & Row, 1968.

Thurman, Howard. *The Creative Encounter*. Richmond, IN: Friends United Press, 1972.

————. *Deep Is the Hunger*. Richmond, IN: Friends United Press, 1973.

————. *Disciplines of the Spirit*. Richmond, IN: Friends United Press, 1977.

————. *Jesus and the Disinherited*. Richmond, IN: Friends United Press, 1981.

————. *The Luminous Darkness*. Richmond, IN: Friends United Press, 1989.

————. *The Search for Common Ground*. Richmond, IN: Friends United Press, 1986.

Uhlein, Gabriele. *Meditations with Hildegard of Bingen*. Santa Fe, NM: Bear & Co., 1982.

Veary, Nana. *Change We Must: My Spiritual Journey*. Honolulu, HI: Institute of Zen Studies, 1989.

Woodruff, Sue. *Meditations with Mechtild of Magdeburg*. Santa Fe, NM: Bear & Co., 1982.

Yockey, James Francis. *Meditations with Nicholas of Cusa*. Santa Fe, NM: Bear & Co., 1987.

PERMISSIONS FOR POETRY
IN *CHRISTIAN MYSTICS*

ABOUT THE AUTHOR

Matthew Fox was a member of the Dominican order for thirty-four years. He holds a doctorate (received summa cum laude) in the History and Theology of Spirituality from the Institut Catholique de Paris. Seeking to establish a pedagogy that was friendly to learning spirituality, he established the Institute in Culture and Creation Spirituality, which operated for seven years at Mundelein College in Chicago and twelve years at Holy Names College in Oakland, California. For ten of those years at Holy Names College, Cardinal Ratzinger (now Pope Benedict XVI), as the Catholic Church's chief inquisitor and head of the Congregation of Doctrine and Faith, tried to shut the program down. Ratzinger silenced Fox for one year in 1988 and forced him to step down as director. Three years later he expelled Fox from the order and aborted the program. Rather than disband his amazing ecumenical faculty, Fox started the University of Creation Spirituality in Oakland, where he was president for nine years.

He is currently a visiting scholar with the Academy for the Love of Learning in Santa Fe, New Mexico. He is working with others to create a new educational experience for inner-city youth called YELLAWE (Youth and Elder Learning Laboratory for Ancestral Wisdom Education). He lectures, teaches, writes, and serves as president of the nonprofit he created in 1984, Friends of Creation Spirituality. He is the author of twenty-eight books and lives in Oakland, California. His website is www.matthewfox.org.